The Black Buddhist

A Spiritual Journey

The Black Buddhist

A Spiritual Journey

Meikle Paschal

Intuitive Press
Boston, Massachusetts

THE BLACK BUDDHIST
A Spiritual Journey
Published by:
Intuitive Press
Boston, Massachusetts
mepas@verizon.net

Meikle Paschal, Publisher / Editorial Director
Yvonne Rose/Quality Press, Production Coordinator
Printed Page, Cover & Text Layout

Photos, courtesy of: The City of Boston Archives, Joseph P. Healey Library, University of Massachusetts/Boston; The South End Historical Society; Brenda Allen; Jacqueline L. McRath; and FLAR Design.

The publication is designed to provide accurate and authoritative information in regard to the subject matter covered. It is sold with the understanding that the Publisher is not engaged in rendering legal or other professional services. If legal advice or other expert assistance is required, the services of a competent professional person should be sought.

Intuitive Press Books are available at special discounts for bulk purchases, sales promotions, fund raising or educational purposes.

ISBN #: 978-0-692-28001-0

Library of Congress Control Number: 2014918528

Second Edition

10 9 8 7 6 5 4 3 2

Dedication

...in memory of My Mother Luella Allen

Acknowledgements

First, I would like to give most sincere and outmost thanks to my wife Marilyn and my children: Kendal, Aleta, Kolette, Zakia and Meikle Jr. (Mikey). In various ways they have all been supportive and enabled me to complete this book. To each of you love and my deepest thanks.

I must acknowledge John Riccio and Sean McCarthy for reading the rough drafts of the manuscript. Both of these gentlemen provided me with insight and encouragement at critical times in the development of this work. Additionally, I want to acknowledge Charlotte Williams who not only read the rough draft of the manuscript but also provided invaluable insight with regard to the development of a special segment of this work.

Special thanks to Florella Orowan, my editor. Without her vision of what this fragmented manuscript could become I would not be at this place. Florella overcame her own scare during a critical point in the formation of this book and continued to work with me on this project. With her steadfast guidance and demand for excellence this manuscript evolved into a piece of work that I am proud to present

I give much thanks to the West Lexington Buddhist group of which I am a member. My group unknowingly was the sounding board for many of the ideas expressed in this book. Also, they supported me in many ways both obvious and not so obvious during this long process.

Thank you to Tony and Yvonne Rose, who, with the Quality Press team dedicated many hours to enlightening me to all the benefits of self-publishing and for reformatting the second edition of my book. Your guidance and commitment to excellence has been priceless.

Last, with all humility and appreciation that cannot be expressed in words I acknowledge my dear friend Jacqueline McRath. Jackie read a rough compilation and saw the possibility. She encouraged me to continue writing. I have no idea of how many times she proof read my submissions, made critical comments and provided unwavering support. I would not have grown as a writer without her support… thank you, Jackie.

Contents

Foreword

One might think that I, a white man from a privileged suburban background, and Meik Pascal, a black man from Boston's South End projects, would have little in common, but we share many things: a love of Boston's Franklin Park, a degree in English, and we live in the same town, to name a few. Most important, though, we share something at the core of our humanity.

You have before you the intimate story of a man's journey from self-doubt and isolation to self-mastery and a deeper connection to life itself—an evolution of a single individual. That this transformation should occur against the backdrop of a crime ridden and prejudicial city in the 20/21st Century in the persona of a black man makes it all the more accessible and fascinating.

Meik and I share a desire to comprehend the universe in which we live and to achieve a genuinely human existence within it, not just as observers, but as participants. We seek to overcome our limitations, to realize our, greatest potentials, and to become our full selves.

We have found in Buddhism a vehicle to accelerate and, indeed, to assure this journey, and it is a privilege to have found a friend with whom to share the ride.

— Ken Loomis
Lexington, MA

Introduction

When I wrote *The Black Buddhist*, I wanted to share my experience as a Black man practicing Nicherin Buddhism as a spiritual belief. I found that my practice dramatically improved the quality of my life and provided a framework out of which to develop a deeper understanding of who I am in this existence. For the many of us wandering and disenchanted with what mainstream Western religions offer, Buddhism presents an attractive and fulfilling alternative.

At this time, *The Black Buddhist* has been read and reviewed by a much larger population than practicing Buddhists and those exploring Buddhism. As a result of the many interviews, lectures and readings that are a part of getting the messages presented in this book to the public, unexpected feedback has emerged. At first the questions were about the rigors of practicing Buddhism. Some of the questions asked probed deeper into my understanding of the Buddhist practice. In addition, many of the questions sought to cast me as some sort of anomaly. In hindsight, many of these questions came from the first people to read my book, my Buddhist family.

But, as time went on, the readers expanded to include the general population and college students. *The Black Buddhist* has been adopted by a number of professors teaching college classes. The classes included Critical Thinking, English, English Literature, Composition and Philosophy. The feedback and questions began to include queries about topics presented in the book relevant to, but beyond Buddhism.

Often feedback focused on my experience growing up in the projects in the Roxbury section of Boston. Many readers expressed common experiences such as those presented. Younger readers currently existing in conditions, such as I, said they were inspired after reading the book with regard to improving their lot in life. Participants in Memoire workshops said they gained renewed enthusiasm to complete stalled writing projects.

More often, the questions focused on the impact of education on my life. The support I received from my mother is frequently explored. Social climbing seems to be of interest to many of the readers. The topic of unexpected support seems to fascinate readers. Needless to say, the central topic of a Black man's experience as a Buddhist is foremost; but the emerging topics of interest have added much more depth to the intermingling of ideas presented.

PART I

The Buddha in Me

I am listening to the sound of my feet on the 2.5-mile cross-country trail through Franklin Park, where I have jogged for more than twelve years. Along the way, I see familiar faces running and walking, seeking the same thing: better health. The trail is challenging, often used for cross-country running events. My route skirts the William Devine Golf Course, sections of which are sporadically lined with a variety of mature oak and birch trees, untrimmed bushes, and a modest bridge spanning Scarboro Pond.

The Franklin Park Jogging Path

Franklin Park is the last and largest component of Frederick Law Olmstead's Emerald Necklace and considered its "crown jewel." In recent years, owing to inner-city crime and a change in the complexion of local residents, the area has been unfortunately neglected and its beauty forgotten. But during the solitude of my runs I have sometimes been distracted by the vegetation's sweet smell or a stunning, colorful vista that has survived the years of neglect.

During one of these captivating moments, I experienced an epiphany that marked a milestone in my life. The mild wind, sweet smell of echinacea and vibrant colors of black-eyed Susans, hypnotic patter of runners' steps and rhythmic breathing inspired a thought: I am a part of all of this — physically, spiritually, and emotionally.

I wondered if my essence lingered in the air through time. What about the me who ran here yesterday, and what about others who have traveled here? Did their vapor also linger and if so, for how long? Maybe it lingers forever in a kind of layering, like an onion. I realized I had become a part of Franklin Park and it was a part of me.

Such moments have the potential of leading one's life in a totally unexpected direction. I wondered if anyone had studied such occurrences, wrote about them, and explained them. More significantly, I wondered if this is what Siddhartha Buddha experienced, sitting under the Bodhi tree 2,500 years ago. I wonder if it took him 40 days and nights of in-depth contemplation or whether he understood it instantly and the rest of the time was devoted to determining how to present his enlightenment. Did he realize the magnitude of his enlightenment and the impact its disclosure would have on the world? Was my own epiphany a revelation of the Buddha in me?

You're Special

My mother used to say, "You're special."

I would ask her, "What makes me special?" and she would say, "That old white doctor… he took his time during your delivery, looked at you and said, 'This one is special'." It seemed to be a defining moment in her life. For me, it had less to do with ego than it did with finding meaning.

My mother Luella Paschal at the age of 21

I said, "Ma, I don't know what you mean. I tell my own children they're special. Why do you keep saying this?" She said, "There are many other things I could tell you Meikle, but you wouldn't believe me. Only that, when you were born, that doctor saw something.

I was born at Boston City Hospital. According to my birth certificate I was born live on June 23, 1950 at 3:00 p. m. My mother, Luella Mae Paschal, is listed as "colored." It was only when she lay on her deathbed, stricken by the complications of diabetes, that I really pressed her on the issue of being "special." She didn't give me an answer.

Some months later, she appeared in my bedroom and sat at the edge of my bed, which sagged under her weight. She looked about forty, healthy and was wearing one of her colorful housecoats. She smiled as she spoke to me with a message of comfort and reassurance. Immediately afterward, I woke up feeling calm as never before. I sat at the edge of my bed, overwhelmed with life's mystery and wept. I realized I was not alone. My mother was still with me.

I wondered about my other ancestors. Were they also still around? Did they play a part in my life? Could they be accessed? Was there some relationship with them that I could still have? Are there others who have been with me, or I with them, throughout endless lifetimes? Have we been watching and supporting one another in this journey? My mother's visit left me with the feeling my mission in life was unfolding before me.

Everything in a Name

My first name is pronounced "Michael" and my last name is pronounced "Pascal." My middle name is Eugene. Over the course of my life I have heard quite a variety of mispronunciations. Your name says a lot about you. It can identify you as a member of a particular group. It can reveal where you come from and your socioeconomic status. It may even reveal your religion and the era in which you were born. You may have a popular name, such as Brittany, Taneesha, Malcolm or Madonna. Names can be given as intended predictors of future occupations, such as: lawyer, judge or senator. Frequently, names are repeated through generations of a family. If you ever asked your parents, "Why did I get stuck with this name?" you may have been told that it belonged to an ancestor and that you should be proud.

Meikle Eugene Paschal at the age of two

My name has served many purposes in my life. For one thing, it does not betray my socioeconomic heritage. It does not reveal my age. It also shields me from racial identification. Over the years, I have come to believe that one reason my resume has not been moved to the bottom of the pile was that it did not identify my race. The fact is that racial profiling in the workplace and school system is unfortunately a common occurrence. Even now, someone named "Jahiem," "Jackson" or "Washington" may be less likely to get an interview or acceptance letter. I often reflect on the scrutiny a resume or application with a common Muslim name must receive. This is unfortunate, and undoubtedly some people are able to rise above the stereotyping, but many more continue the practice that impacts on increasingly-competitive school and job opportunities.

The name Paschal, an Old Testament reference to the first Passover, belonged to my maternal grandfather, which reveals significant sensitive information about me: my mother and father were not married. Truthfully, I've always found this embarrassing, although it does not define me as a person.

William Boyd Paschal was from Henderson, South Carolina. I know nothing more about him or his family but that he was a railroad porter in the early twentieth century. When the genealogical craze arose in my family, we chose to focus on the lineage of my maternal grandmother. How my grandfather's family came to be named Paschal has yet to be uncovered.

I was named after my uncle, Alfred Eugene Meikle Paschal, my maternal grandmother's first child who was born on April 8, 1920. In the early 1900s, my maternal grandmother, Aida Virginia Williams, moved to Boston from Claremont, NH. She took a room at 618 Shawmut Avenue in Boston, then lived in Cambridge for awhile before moving to Roxbury's Oakburn Avenue. The 1919 census revealed that she was known as "Aida Meikle" and that Alfred's father was from the British West Indies. I have not been able to discover whether she was married to someone named

Meikle because it has been impossible to find a marriage certificate. Somewhere around the same time, William and Aida met and were married on June 16, 1921. My uncle Alfred, however, remains somewhat of a mystery.

As a child, I never thought to ask questions about my name. By the time I did, I was in mid-adolescence and the family members who would have known had already died, except for my mother. The obvious question was to ask her, but I knew that to press her on certain issues would start a needless argument and not get any information.

Left: William Henry Paschal, my maternal grandfather, about 1922
Right: My maternal grandmother, Aida V. Paschal

Moreover, I had become used to my name and to my uncle being a mystery. I had grown up with these realities, so there was no real urgency. By the time the answers had become more important, it was too late. My mother was by then in her early sixties and had come to forgetfulness early. When I asked her about family history, she would struggle to remember, then simply give up.

As a child I would occasionally see the name "Meikle" in the strangest places. One day I was reading a list of doctors' names inscribed on a brass plaque in front of Boston City Hospital and saw that one of them had my name. From then on, whenever I was in the neighborhood I would return to the plaque, just to read my name. It was a validation that I did not have some made-up name, because it had also been given to someone of a high rank. Years later, I was surprised when reading the credits for the "Mary Tyler Moore Show" that someone listed there also had my name.

In the early years of computer search engines I was teaching a graduate class in Advanced Research in Education. I began the course as usual by explaining the pronunciation of my names. This was one of my classroom "icebreakers," to explain that "Paschal" was from the Old Testament and that "Meikle" is the correct way to spell "Michael." I concluded by joking that it was a conspiracy, that parents planning to name their child "Michael" should spell it correctly!

After class, several students told me they had found my name through a Dogpile search, under "Ode to Meikle," an ancient Scottish poem. I subsequently went to some Scottish sites looking for the name Meikle and emailed everyone with that name, asking whether I was spelling it correctly, whether it was pronounced "Michael," what was its history and anything else they could tell me.

The response was overwhelming. I was told that I was indeed pronouncing it correctly, but only because of some war fought in antiquity over the correct pronunciation. Apparently those who pronounced it "Michael" had won. I imagine the "war" actually consisted of three or four guys in a pub with too much to drink, rather than columns of armored soldiers facing off on a hill.

As it happened my uncle, Sgt. Alfred Eugene Meikle Paschal, was killed in action in Korea on March 9, 1951. By doing research online and with the aid of military documents I was able to see pictures of his place of death in Korea but have as yet been unable to locate his birthplace or birth certificate.

Such mysteries exist in most families, and the deaths of those who hold the answers take that knowledge to the grave, and the questions linger for the survivors hungry for enlightenment and closure. In reality, however, frequently such mysteries should remain so, because the answers may bring problems, pain and suffering.

Oakburn Avenue

Boston's Oakburn Avenue, known as "Oakie," was a nostalgic turn-of-the-century neighborhood where the old-timers sat all day by their windows, listening to the radio and watching life outside. The street was a row of dark brown clapboard houses, their cracks and missing sections showing their age — relics that had hung on long after their time. Occasionally an entire building would be missing, like an extracted front tooth. These three-story wood frame houses were divided into cold-water flats without central heating. The huge black coal stove in the kitchen never really heated the bedrooms or living room. Those were warmed by kerosene space heaters, deadly if left unsupervised. The wooden stairs leading to the top floors had been a carrying route for coal, wood and kerosene for countless decades. Sometimes, a carelessly-discarded cigarette would ignite the kerosene-soaked stairs, causing a raging house fire. In the alleyways, the trash barrels gave off the stench of garbage.

An example of the Oakburn Avenue apartment building hallway.
Owing to urban renewal, the neighborhood no longer exists.

Those were the days when everyone was young — cousins, brothers and sisters lived and played together. Grandmother was alive, uncles and aunts were vital and good-looking. Christmas had a special meaning and summer seemed to last forever.

In these memories we tend to forget about the drunken uncle staggering about. We don't immediately recall the Sunday morning when a mentally ill woman walked up and down the street, screaming that she had been sexually assaulted the night before, or the young man who was taken away in handcuffs after running all the way home. These dark, ugly realities get lost in our memories of childhood.

In this neighborhood between Oakburn Avenue and Haskins Street was the West End Hub and Spring Factory, which produced bedsprings and bed frames. When I was 15, I got a summer job there, working with my uncle Eugene. The factory was a cold, drafty deathtrap of creaking wooden floors and open-geared machinery, driven by an overhead leather-strapped drive shaft. It had been the workplace of Polish immigrants before the black workers showed up. At the end of the workday, large drums of kerosene were used to wash off the metal dust and aluminum paint. Whiskey and wine kept my uncles warm and singing as they worked.

To me, Oakburn Avenue and the West End Hub and Spring Factory were the equivalent of a Northern plantation. The employees lived in the vicinity of the factory. Every morning, a factory whistle announced the start of the work day. Another at midday told them to take lunch, and a third in the evening signaled that it was time to go home.

In the early evening when I went to Al Green's corner store I would see my uncles, along with the other factory workers, standing around sharing a bottle in a brown paper bag. After years of drinking on the job and after work, three of my uncles died of alcoholism. I doubt that any of those workers earned enough to escape the brutal factory life or the squalor that was the reality of "Oakie."

I'm the oldest of four children, with one brother and two sisters. My mother Luella was an attractive, heavy-set woman with no more than an eighth-grade education, although she read a lot, mostly romance novels. She was briefly married and would now be described as a "single parent." Yet somehow, by herself and with limited resources, when I was five years old she managed to engineer our escape from Oakburn Avenue and we moved up the social ladder to the Lenox Street Housing Development, also known as The Projects.

Lenox Street

In 1938, Massachusetts Governor Charles F. Hurley signed the Massachusetts Housing Authority Act. This was a part of the WPA initiative, although his ceremonial remarks at the signing made little reference to low income housing. The project was one of several designed to redevelop an aging city and accommodate a growing population. At the time, the City of Boston was in a state of decline. Some residential buildings had no indoor plumbing, and it was commonplace for a five-story brick building inhabited by 20 families to have one communal bathroom per floor. The city still had stables, outhouses and buildings with no central heating. In the downtown area, prostitution was rampant and it was not uncommon to see drunken sailors wandering in and out of local nightclubs. Along with this squalor came crime.

The Lenox Street Housing Development

At first, the housing developments were the homes of Greek, Syrian, Italian and other-newly-arrived immigrants in Boston's South End. Over time, the projects became the refuge not only for low-income whites but an increasing number of low-income blacks. Somewhat later, the housing developments became the exclusive domain of low-income blacks. In 1955, my family moved to the Lenox Street housing development.

When we arrived, the project was a safe, well-kept place. It was divided into segments called "courts." Each court was named after a prominent African-American resident of Ward 9. Trotter Court was named for the political activist and founder of the Guardian newspaper, William Monroe Trotter. Lattimore Court was named for the famous black physician and politician Dr. Andrew Lattimore. Ditmus Court was named for Civil War veteran Edward A. Ditmus, who may have been politically active in Ward 9. Every court had swings and slides and each end of the Lenox Street Projects had a wading pool. These remained in use for some years.

By the mid-1940s, when Lenox Street Housing Development was probably completed, someone had named the courts after notable African-Americans. At that time, the South End was a poor but racially diverse area. Years later, I realized the racial significance of the courts' names and that began to intrigue me. Was it sending a signal that the inhabitants would eventually be predominately African-American? And who in the politically-patronaged Boston Housing Authority of the 1930s and '40s would have had the license to choose such names?

Lenox Street had resident youth gangs, although their names seemed more colorful than dangerous. There were the Marquise, the Junior Marquise, The Undertakers, and The Marce Dukes. The Undertakers wore black capes with red velvet linings with their names and emblems written across the back. At that time, in the late 1950s, I was too young to understand or be affected by the gangs.

When these gang members finally grew up, started families, went to jail or were killed, their successors metamorphosed into something worse. Some of these individuals became career criminals, like the young bully who lived in Lattimore. Each individual had a group of followers and each group was a gang. Each project or area had its own gang and they were all dangerous. Since I was from the South End, I could not safely go to another project or part of town because I did not belong to a gang and it was too dangerous.

Although it would have been easy to join a gang as protection I had seen too many young men get their faces slashed with razors, shot by small caliber pistols, and beaten severely. I was on my own, without the protection of a father, older brother or cousin. Whether from the fear of getting hurt, the possibility of arrest and juvenile detention or simply family training, I somehow escaped gang life.

To stay safe, I used a variety of tactics. Sometimes I would run home from school, or take a deviated route to get home. I had many close calls and could have easily become a statistic. Looking back on it, I wonder if I was being protected, if those experiences were somehow necessary for me to develop into who I am today. As a Buddhist, I wonder if it was an exercise in some unfinished learning from a previous life.

Karma works in mysterious ways. Other young men, similar to me in affect and attitude, never made it home from the party. One, a friend nicknamed "Mouse" for his unassuming demeanor, was stabbed to death for accidentally stepping on a gang member's foot while dancing. Senseless killings such as his were common.

In the early 1960s, however, a number of social and political conditions converged to change everything. Many young men who lived in the projects went to Viet Nam and either did not return or returned violent and strung out on heroin. Some of those returning veterans spearheaded an epidemic of heroin addiction in the projects that still exists. Those of us who stayed home discovered marijuana. I had just turned 14 when on the Saint Emmanuel settlement house basketball court one summer day I smoked pot for the first time. This later became a habit that had a deleterious effect on my life for years afterward.

In 1967 a film called *Titicut Follies* exposed the inhumane treatment of patients in Massachusetts' mental health institutions. Under pressure, the Commonwealth began releasing patients, giving housing priority to those who had previously been confined. Soon afterward, the projects became even more dangerous. Drugs, robberies, and incidents involving mental patients became more common. The project's swings and slides disappeared and the wading pools ceased to work.

Bluebirds and Robins

The South End's grammar schools had been built during the Civil War. They were of red brick construction and most of the teachers were white. I attended the Hyde Elementary School, located on Hammond Street. Throughout my entire elementary school education, I saw only two black teachers, one man and one woman, and neither returned the following year. Before class, the students would line up outside in the play area. Those who were already being tracked as "bright" were labeled as either Bluebirds or Robins and were separated from the students placed in lower groups. I was either a Bluebird or a Robin.

The Hyde Elementary School just before its demolition

After that, I attended the Sherwin Middle School on Sterling Street. Our textbooks were old, torn and tattered, with 4- or 5-line labels on which you wrote your name. All my books had at least two labels with every line filled. Some students would try to get the same copies their older siblings had used. The course work was rote memorization, with long lines of addition and subtraction followed by long lines of multiplication and division. The curriculum was designed to be a preparation for employment in the trades — plumbing, carpentry or possibly as an electrician.

The Sherwin Middle School on Sterling Street in Roxbury

This was the beginning of the Civil Rights movement and the Freedom Bus Rides, when many poor, uneducated Negroes from the South moved north to escape sharecropping and segregation. When these boys arrived at our school, they were immediately placed a grade or two below their age level, so by the time I was in eighth grade some of my classmates looked more like young men than boys. Sometimes after dropping out of school, they would return to class in Army uniforms.

I was very unhappy in this environment. As a tall, thin, light-skinned youth I got into a lot of fights. The darker boys wanted to see my face turn red or get bruised. Not only my peers provoked me but the older boys also joined in. After a few fights, running home lost its shame. These fights, although not an everyday occurrence, happened often enough to make school miserable. One day Mr. DeCosta, our homeroom teacher, announced that anyone interested in taking the "exam school" test would be released at half-day. Although I did not understand exactly what that was, I left to take the test — anything to get out of the classroom.

It was a test for admission to Boston Technical High School, one of the most prestigious public high schools in Boston. To my surprise, not only did I pass but I passed at a high level. I had attended segregated project schools staffed by disinterested teachers and had no preparation for the exam. No one had encouraged or prompted me. I could have very easily skipped it but when Mr. DeCosta made the announcement, I was suddenly very "present." How could this be? The opportunity to escape an inferior education had presented itself and, in retrospect, this made all the difference in my life.

Remembering that decisive moment, I sometimes awakened in the early morning in a panic state, thinking, *Where would I be now if I had not made the right choice?* The decision to take a test totally unprepared was, in essence, the decision to take a chance. Looking back, I wonder if the experience was guided by protective forces, whether it was a part of my mission unfolding, since school, education and guidance have been central to my professional life.

University of Massachusetts

I was unprepared for Boston Technical High. The transition from a segregated, impoverished middle school to a nearly all-white, well-equipped high school with high standards was a shock. Consequently, I began hanging out with a mixed group of students who studied little but smoked a lot of pot. It was the psychedelic 1960s, and among this disenfranchised group, long hair, bell-bottom pants and platform shoes accompanied a lack of any real planning for the future. Then suddenly, the adult world materialized in the form of the Viet Nam War and I realized the significance of the Trailways buses outside the recruitment center across the street from Dudley Station. From my perspective, going to Viet Nam meant certain death.

The former Boston Technical High School, now the home of the Boston Latin Academy

Soon after my high school graduation, I received a draft notice. It was the usual "greetings" letter and I was instructed to report to the induction center. On the way to my physical, I saw guys from my neighborhood, guys from middle school and a few high school friends, all headed in the same direction. As we returned to the Trailways bus station, I thought about how humiliating and impersonal the entire process had been: standing in long lines in your underwear, a flashlight shined up your butt, fingers stuck in your testicles as you turned your head and coughed. All the while, I was thinking how I should have made plans for life after high school. I stepped off the bus, lost in deep thought.

Suddenly I realized I was standing in front of a University of Massachusetts building, so I went inside. What happened next is little more than a haze. Somehow I made my way through the corridors to the admissions center and interviewed with a student recruiter, whom I remember as very preppy. I wasn't intimidated or afraid. I had taken the pre-SAT and SATs and have always done well on standardized tests. My scores were well above average. Sometime later, the recruiter who had interviewed me said that the combination of my test scores and my interview got me admitted.

In my despondency I could have easily walked down the street, gotten on the Arlington Street trolley and returned home. This is another moment in my life on which I have reflected many times. An unexpected opportunity presented itself and I embraced it. I believe that both opportunity and disaster were present in that moment and, without hesitation, I embraced the opportunity. I was starting to see a pattern in these moments. I could hear my mother's voice in my ear, giving me guidance. Even at a time when my understanding of such things was scattered and chaotic, a path ahead was made for me.

The University of Massachusetts / Boston Library aka "The Castle", in the 1970s

How often in life do we make decisions based on fear? Fear is more potent than any drug, and can be just as addictive. It is a debilitating emotion that prevents us from reaching our full potential. Fear causes feelings of inadequacy, which results in settling for less. Chronic fear will cause you to stay within your comfort zone, never venturing beyond the familiar. In Buddhist thought, fear represents a fundamental darkness, representing a weakness to be overcome. I am happy to say that as an adult, I have confronted my fear and no longer experience the nagging sensation that dogged my footsteps in my youth. It has not gone away, but I have managed to keep it under control. In moments of weakness or impulse, however, the demon can re-emerge.

Skip Parties and Gang Bangers

At sixteen, I left home. I did not sever ties with my family but I spent very little time there. The Lenox Street Housing Development had become too dangerous. I was still in high school and getting good grades. I had not dropped out or gone to reform school and was not a part of a gang. Therefore, I was an outsider in the neighborhood and had consequently become a target.

A high school friend had gotten an apartment in a burned-out building near Dudley Station. Its owner was a physician who performed illegal abortions and obviously realized the building would soon be torn down. For six months, he let it out to us rent free. All we had to do was to clean the apartment.

For a while, things went well. Friends stopped by with wine and weed, our music was loud and girls magically appeared. We were close to Dudley Station, a major bus and train terminal in lower Roxbury. All day long, thousands of people hustled through the station, including students making transit connections. Therefore, Dudley became the place where students skipping school would gather to determine where the "skip party" was going to be. Many days, it was at our apartment. We kept the boys to a minimum, only inviting the girls.

Some of the teenagers hanging out at Dudley Station were "gang bangers" who made their livelihoods robbing people in and around the station. They were very aware of traffic in and around the station, so it was only a matter of time before they noticed a group of students skipping school and heading somewhere.

One day shortly after the party started, two of the most notorious of these thugs kicked down the door. Pandemonium broke out.

They grabbed two girls and demanded sex. One girl said, "I'm on my period" and was let go. The other girl refused and was viciously beaten. Everyone else fled while the gang bangers were focused on the two girls. I ran away and never went back to that apartment.

From that rat-infested dump I moved in with other roommates in North Cambridge. This apartment was clean, large and on a quiet side street in a safe neighborhood. One of my new roommates was a "trip master"—someone who orchestrated field trips and excursions along Commonwealth Ave. and the Charles River of small groups who were dropping LSD. My other roommate was escaping a heroin-addicted mother.

I was living there when the draft induction letter arrived at my mother's house. I would have stayed there longer but during one of our many drug parties, an apparently-unstable girl went into a closet and slit her wrists. Fortunately, she survived but the event caused a lot of tension between the roommates. After this experience, I called my mother for advice and she told me to come home immediately.

For six months, I slept on the living room couch. The couch was uncomfortable enough, but family members would get up during the night to go to the refrigerator or to use the bathroom. In the mornings after my brother left for school, I would sneak into his bedroom to get some rest. Having experienced life in a middle-class, racially-mixed neighborhood, returning to Lenox Street was painful.

While at the University of Massachusetts I ran into my friend Reggie. He was about two years older than I and was a poor relation of a wealthy family. He was 6'5," wore thick glasses and was not very good-looking. When still in high school, I had met him while working in the kitchen at Peter Bent Brigham Hospital. Because he looked old enough to buy liquor, I would get him to buy a bottle of Bacardi Light rum before heading out to a party. Reggie was from the Cathedral Projects in Boston's South End. It had a slightly better reputation than Lenox but was also dangerous. Reggie had moved out to live with his pregnant girlfriend, but their relationship ended and he soon found himself back at home with his mother, desperately wanting to get out.

The neighborhood in Roxbury during the 1970s.
Much of this part of Boston has since been the focus of urban renewal.

The University of Massachusetts at Boston is a non-residential commuter campus with mostly college-age students and a few continuing education and ex-military older adults. Getting room-mates to share the rent was critical and many of the newly-enrolled students were competing for roommates, so I quickly located Reggie as a potential candidate. We became roommates during our first semester at UMass Boston and shared various apartments for almost five years thereafter.

One good thing about being a starving college student is that you most likely receive financial aid, either in the form of grants or loans. The financial aid package is comprised of cash, intended to help you pay your tuition, but may also include a work-study job, usually on the campus. Additionally, you may be able to get a summer job, either on- or off-campus. The summer job may be an internship, related to the field you plan to pursue when you leave college.

The University of Massachusetts / Boston "campus" in the 1970s. As evident in the photo, it was in the midst of downtown Boston.

Working full time with a full course load and maintaining an apartment while doing a lot of drugs was a challenge. Often we would move out within six months, having only paid the first month's rent and fees. After avoiding the landlord for as long as possible, we would leave late at night or on a weekend. I had spent most of my savings on my half of the rent and security deposit. I had never been this low on money and was consequently nervous. Reggie seemed unconcerned because at least we had an apartment and college was about to begin. I was anticipating some financial aid in the form of loans, grants, and a work-study job. My plan was to get an on-campus job but would not be getting a pay check for a couple of weeks.

Everything went well until I learned that my financial aid was going to be delayed. Eating and transportation were causing my limited funds to dwindle. Eventually, I reached the point where I had no food or money and Reggie had disappeared. I was all alone with my hunger. After two days of nothing to eat, all my thoughts centered on food. I tried to distract myself but the rumbling in my stomach always brought my thoughts back to food.

On Friday, I hit rock bottom. I had no classes that day and living off-campus meant I was far away from any kind of school support. I got nervous to the point of panicking... it was a struggle to maintain control. I was burning energy and feeling weak. I slept as much as I could, thinking I could sleep all the way to the arrival of the financial aid.

Then I got the idea of filling my stomach with water, thinking it might make the hunger go away. I started drinking glasses—actually, jars—of water whenever my stomach started growling. Ultimately, I found myself sticking my head under the faucet in the kitchen sink. I drank so much water I could feel my stomach tightening.

I could feel the water slogging around in my stomach, but I was still hungry. I was shocked when the water did not make the hunger go away. Despondent, I left the apartment and began walking up and down Blue Hill Avenue. I felt a sharp pain behind my knees. At times, my legs trembled as I walked, and my steps became labored. I manually picked up my feet and placed them one in front of the other.

I found myself standing in front of a neighborhood diner commonly referred to as a "greasy spoon." It appeared to be empty. There was a brown skinned older woman behind the counter who had the aura of being from the South. She had a white scarf tied around her head with a wing knot in the front and wore a white blouse and a white apron. The image of her will always be embedded in my memory.

The area around Dudley Station in Roxbury.
The elevated train tracks have since been torn down.

In my most humble voice, I confessed to this stranger, "Ma'am, I have not eaten in two days." She produced a plate on which were two pork chop sandwiches. The white bread was soaked with the grease from the pork chops. I am embarrassed to say that I ate the sandwiches and only said, "thank you." I was not even thoughtful enough to offer to wash dishes or provide any other service for her kindness. Since that time, I have tried to make amends by helping someone else in need when the situation presents itself.

Soon after that incident, I learned that the school financial aid office was giving emergency loans to bridge the time until the student loans arrived, but I learned a significant lesson from this painful situation and have never allowed myself or anyone around me to go hungry again.

The Fight — Girl Gangs

In my senior year of college, I got a summer work-study job at the Roxbury Multi-service Center Community Settlement House, called the "fire house." It was located directly across the street from my former high school. Behind the settlement house was a vacant lot where student fights took place — often between black and white students. Because the school was predominantly white, I had witnessed quite a few fights.

In the heat of the skirmish, racial slurs would flood the air, often starting additional fights. Knives were sometimes pulled out of schoolbags. The fights were particularly vicious, as if the participants were being forced to defend their race, birth country or ethnicity. Sometimes, school officials would come racing to the back of the settlement house to haul the students away. When I started working there, memories of those tense times resurfaced.

Now, however, rather than high school students, the participants were members of rival gangs. These were not the flamboyant, older teenage gangs of the 1950s and early 1960s but rather middle school students, ages 10 to 15, from the neighborhood, many of whom had long, serious criminal records. They were obviously from poor families and dressed in haphazard fashion. Some did not look very clean. Many of them carried guns.

Two separate gangs used the place as a hangout. Although "gangs" might seem an exaggeration for such young combatants, these groups had a distinct hierarchy, a leader, and operated as a unit. The first group consisted of young boys whose leader looked like he was asleep, his eyes barely open. He was small, thin and brown-skinned with an aura of being dangerous. His inner circle consisted of three or four boys, with three or four others more loosely connected to the group.

A current-day photo of the Roxbury Multi-service Youth Center, front view.

The second gang consisted of girls, with a hierarchy similar to the boys'— an identifiable leader, inner circle and several more loosely-affiliated members. Their leader was also poorly-dressed and had poor hygiene. She was not particularly tall but had a muscular build—not bad-looking, but not very feminine-looking either, as were her subordinates.

15a.A current-day photo of the Roxbury Multi-service Youth Center, side view.

These gang members all appeared to be marginalized. I cannot imagine any of them holding a school office, being involved in sports or in a school play. In fact, school was probably not a positive experience for any of them and the settlement house had become their refuge. On the streets, around the community, and particularly at the settlement house, they had value and they had a voice.

I had only been there a few days when I witnessed my first fight. I saw the familiar circle of spectators — a telltale fight sign, with a smaller circle of bodies forcing the combatants into the middle. I was frightened and didn't know what to do. From my Lenox Street days, I had witnessed Good Samaritans get stabbed and even killed in trying to break up fights. The two gang leaders were circling each other, sizing each other up. That's when I really got scared, because I knew the girl was going to get severely beaten. In these situations, the crowd generally provokes the fight. When a girl is involved, her blouse gets ripped off and her breasts exposed, to the delight of the onlookers. There is no escape for the participants, no running away.

Then suddenly, the girl executed a classic street-fighting technique. In a way, it was a thing of beauty to witness. She "scooped" the boy; that is, she rushed him, grabbed him around the ankles and flipped him into the air. It was a perfectly-executed move, resulting in a stunning coup. The boy seemed to rise several feet into the air, came down on his arm and began to scream. Undeterred, the girl jumped on him, punching him until her arms appeared to get tired. This all took place within 10 or 15 seconds, then the girls faded down the street and around the corner.

I do not remember seeing the girl gang leader again but the boy was back the next day with a cast on his arm. It had been broken in the fight. His gang members were very vocal in his defense, saying that he was tired and that's why she was able to scoop him. However, there was a softer subtext that said, "No. She beat his ass and broke his arm." Afterward, things seemed to go on as normal at the settlement house. I guess I was the only one shaken by the event.

Late Bloomer

These gang members were my constituency at the settlement house summer job. I was very nervous that in some way, I might transgress some unknown barrier, offend one of them and be attacked on my way home. That summer was tense and I was always on my guard. My job was to provide recreational programs for teenagers with all-too-much time on their hands. I organized activities such as trips to the park, to the skating rink and to the beach. The settlement house provided the usual facilities for ping-pong, football, and had a broken-down basketball hoop in the back. The game of choice was basketball, which also happened to generate the most fights.

Meikle at the age of 23

In order to be effective at our jobs, summer staffers were required to get training from the support staff funding the settlement house, which meant occasional trips to the branch office. One day, several older ladies arrived to give us a ride. Without thinking, I sat in the middle of the back seat, over the driveshaft hump. With my long legs, it was very uncomfortable, and I sat there, wondering how I could have been so stupid as to not take a window seat.

I was so distracted by discomfort that I barely noticed when one of the women in front turned around and spoke to me. I can still remember her face, the color of her hair, and particularly her eyes. She spoke as if we were the only two people present and she was channeling vital information that would impact my future. She said, "You're just like my dead husband. He was a late bloomer also." She turned back and did not speak again, but her words have stayed with me ever since. I now wonder if this was another instance of Shoten Zenjin, providing me with vital information to further my development or to help me better understand my mission in life.

Since that incident, I have noticed various instances of delayed development and achievement in my life. For example, I wasted nearly 10 years before I began teaching, despite my interest in pursuing it as a vocation. I also put off going to graduate school for five years. When I decided to teach, it was necessary to return to school to get another undergraduate degree in English. Then, in order to get certified I needed teacher certification classes and to develop a Master's degree in English, all of which required sixteen more courses. I procrastinated another three years before entering the doctoral program, which took eight years of nights and summers to finish.

These delays might have been avoided with some timely guidance but perhaps I wasn't ready, maybe I needed time to develop in other ways. During these years, no one prodded me to continue my schooling or advance my career. I had little or no guidance in making employment or education decisions. No one in my family had worked in white-collar jobs, nor had achieved my level of education. They had praised me and uttered broad platitudes about the merits of advancement, but had given no advice on navigating the pitfalls of a professional job because they didn't have that experience. In my family I was essentially a pioneer, so when I experienced professional missteps, it was based on a lack of preparation or advice that might have otherwise furthered my advancement. I had no grooming and gained insights the hard way. Fortunately, my children, extended family and students have had the benefit of my experience.

Graduation

While living in various off-campus apartments, Reggie and I cultivated a group of "leeches" who would show up at all hours for various self-serving reasons. Some were students still living with their parents, needing somewhere to be alone with their girlfriends. Some wanted to hang out and listen to music but most of them just wanted to smoke dope. Even when I was studying for exams, trying to read or write papers, there was always someone around. Studying under these conditions was difficult.

I had good study habits and liked to read. Even with all the interruptions, I could usually finish my assignments. Of course, with better concentration and more sleep I probably would have done even better. I wondered about the guys who spent long hours in the University's Afro-American Center, drinking Cold Duck, playing Bid Whist and sneaking out the back hallways to smoke a joint. I also wondered about going to class stoned and how that affected one's grades. I wondered about being too stoned to go to class.

At the beginning of the semester I would look at my transcript to see the previous semester's grades. One time, however, I took a closer look. I tallied up the course credit, reviewed my upper level distribution and looked long and hard at my grade point average. I realized that with a full course load and a few more required courses I could graduate in two semesters. What a shock!

I decided to buckle down and graduate but the leeches were relentless. If I was at the school library studying, they would drop by to ask if I had pot and wanted to get high. It seemed that studying was a joke to them. They did not see me as having a purpose in life, they saw me as a resource. Finally, I told them to get the fuck away from me and they got the message. I consequently was regarded as an asshole and they left me alone.

This experience made me realize that during my undergraduate years, I had lost sight of the discipline that was so critical to my earlier education. It had gotten me up in the morning and on the way to class. It had enabled me to get through an elite high school. This was some inner-directed quality that no one had ever encouraged me to develop. I wondered where it had come from, whether it was innate and, most importantly, how to best use it. From these questions, I developed a mantra: "All things are possible with discipline."

The University of Massachusetts/Boston, 1970

One spring day before graduation, I asked a group of about seven guys at the UMass Boston Afro-American Center about their plans. I said, "Are you getting out this term?" Each one answered, "Oh, yeah, or "Hell, yeah." So I said, "What are you doing after the ceremony, maybe we can hook up." They were non-committal, so I suggested Kon Tiki Restaurant, a mid-priced Polynesian-style restaurant in the Prudential building at Copley Square. They seemed agreeable, so we made plans to gather at the restaurant after the ceremony.

The University of Massachusetts/Boston, 1970

Graduation day arrived. When the graduates' names were called to walk across the stage, none of the guys from the Afro-American Center were called — not one! I got my diploma and had my picture taken. My family, including my future wife figured that in all the confusion, we had just missed each other.

Years later, I got together to socialize with a group of about twenty former UMass classmates. As we all sat down for refreshments, somebody asked, "Did anyone ever graduate from that place?" I said, "Yeah, I did!" But I was the only one! As it turned out, no one else at the table had graduated. Some did eventually graduate from college, but I often wonder how I was able to hold things together and succeed under those circumstances. I think I had developed confidence by listening to an internal voice, prodding me to move ahead. I also think that being able to pull away from the crowd made all the difference.

Education, which ultimately became my chosen profession, has been a pillar in my life. Those college years may have represented a pivotal point in my development and I have since often wondered how to share my struggles and that experience with others. The same discipline, I think, enabled me to embrace Buddhist practice more easily and to gain greater understanding of Buddhist thought.

PART II

Getting Straight

I met Marilyn at the home of my cousin William. It was a hot day in June, pre-air conditioning, and one of those moments you never forget. This stunning woman suddenly entered the apartment. Her skin was a beautiful black, her bare arms highlighted by the glistening of a light sweat. I immediately noticed her full, toothy smile and her short Afro. She was wearing stylish blue work overalls with a knit halter top underneath. She had on dark blue John Lennon style peeper sunglasses and moved like a model. The height of this tall, slender woman was enhanced by then-popular platform shoes. My attraction to her was immediate and undeniable.

After graduation we got married and two years later we had a daughter. You might imagine that having a family would have reformed me but in fact, the partying didn't stop — my drinking and smoking marijuana lasted a full ten years after college. This was in the post-Viet Nam years, and jobs were scarce. I realized that in the haze of my college years, I had not prepared for a career. Although I had gone to class and received good grades, I had wasted time with the wrong people, made poor choices and achieved little personal growth.

Teaching appealed to me. During college, I had an opportunity to pursue it but had allowed it to slip away. At one point, I was enrolled in a teacher preparation program but had trouble completing it. On reflection, I think the administrators realized I was involved in too much drinking and drug use. Although I never indulged during training or on site, I think they were able to recognize the lifestyle. Similar opportunities had come about, but for one reason or another I had not taken advantage of them.

Weeks of unemployment turned into months, and the security of student financial aid evaporated. Rent and other living expenses had to be paid. Every day, I applied for jobs, interviewed and waited for phone calls. I wondered if the drinking and drugs showed on my face or were evident in my behavior.

One day on a downtown train, I looked around at the more vulnerable passengers and had a desperate thought: I could just take someone's bag or wallet. Sure they'd be upset at the financial loss but they'd get over it and I needed money now! The very thought of robbing someone scared me but it wouldn't go away. Later that day, I was pounding the pavement downtown looking for work when I walked by a small store on a side street. An old, unmistakably Jewish, shopkeeper remarked as I passed by," If you cut your hair, you'll find a job." I was furious, thinking, *'Who does he think he's talking to…he doesn't know me…racist pig bastard!'*

After several more weeks of being turned down, coming in second or just missing getting hired, I decided to take the shopkeeper's advice: I went to my barbershop. My barber hadn't seen me in years! I could smell the liquor on his breath as we caught up on old times and he cut my Afro into a more conservative hairstyle. I would like to say that the haircut opened many doors, but it did not. It only opened one door — to a demeaning, dead-end insurance job.

The insurance company job was a horror. I sat in a huge room with lines of desks and endless stacks of papers. Other than a thirty-minute lunch break and two ten-minute breaks, my workday was devoted to processing endless insurance applications. One day, I had stomach distress and went to the bathroom. No sooner had I returned to my desk than I needed to dash back. Soon after, my supervisor came up to me, saying I had gone to the bathroom too often!

The situation was ridiculous and inhumane. The longtime employees didn't like me because I was a college graduate and they felt I didn't deserve the salary I was making. I hated the job so much that, during my four years there, I used all my personal and vacation time to look for a better job. I hated it so much that I would get upset on Sunday evening because the next day, I had to go to work. Then I started getting upset on Saturday evening because the next day was Sunday! Since I now had a family, I needed the money and couldn't quit. Finally, I landed a job.

On one of my lunch breaks, I went to an interview at the Department of Youth Services (usually referred to as "DYS"), located in a municipal building across from the Boston Juvenile Court. The room was hazy with dust swirling in the air, highlighted by shafts of sunlight. I was introduced to ten or twelve people sitting around a large table. I scanned their faces, trying to make eye contact and remember their names, but there were too many people. One man and one woman, both African-American, appeared to be conducting the interview.

I answered all their questions with what I believed were appropriate answers. Then I was asked a question that stopped me cold. This was another of those moments that I have come to recognize as a pivotal point in my life. I often wonder if this recognition is some force in nature guiding and protecting me. In Nichiren Buddhism this is referred to as Shoten Zenjin: those powers in the universe that serve to protect us.

The entire interview could hinge on my response to this question. In what seemed like a lifetime, I contemplated whether to give an honest or safe answer. The safe answer could be seen as disingenuous and might cost me the job. But the honest answer was also risky.

One of the interviewers, a young white man, asked what I would do if a client called me a nigger. I said, "It depends whether the client is black or white." He asked me to explain. I said, "As a black man, if a white client referred to me as a nigger he had crossed many boundaries, was taking a chance, and certainly was being hostile. On the other hand, a black client might be trying to establish familiarity and bond with me." Later, I was told that answer nearly cost me the job. The black woman, who apparently had some authority, had intervened and explained my response in more detail. My unconventional choice had proven successful and I was hired.

As a result, four years of handling insurance applications was followed by six years of working with juvenile delinquents. Some had simply lost their way and gotten into trouble but most of my clients were thugs and bullies. They made me uncomfortable, because they reminded me of the gangbangers I had avoided in the Lenox Street projects. In addition, the salary was so low that I had to take other part-time jobs at night and on week-ends.

In spite of that, it was a full ten years after graduation before I decided to live without intoxicants. I was never a heavy drinker because I had discovered early in life that I had a low tolerance for alcohol and when I got drunk, things could get ugly. But for twenty years, I had smoked pot on a daily basis. I would have a joint the first thing in the morning and the last thing at night. I had demons — childhood memories that the marijuana held at bay until I was able to fall asleep. I would like to say that those demons are now gone but that would not be completely true. At the same time, I no longer need marijuana to fall asleep.

I needed to make a major change, so I decided to live my life completely free from drugs and alcohol. I had tried it several times before but had failed. Friends, some whom had never previously had their own weed or beer, would suddenly appear, offering the best of both. This time, however, I decided to isolate myself from everyone but my wife and children. In reflecting on that decision, I realized I had used the same approach when I was trying to finish college. It seemed to work for me.

First, I stopped drinking. That was easy. Next, I announced to my family that I was going to stop smoking pot. That was hard because I was still hanging out with Reggie, my friend from college days. Because we had shared apartments and had gone through so much together, Reggie was like a brother to me. One day at

Houghton's Pond, I ran into him and another friend and they asked the usual question: "Got anything to smoke?" I told them, "Hey man, I just quit." Their reaction was, "So, now what're you gonna do?" No "Congratulations, that's a good thing" or any other positive feedback.

The Trotter Court in the Lenox Housing Project. My bedroom was the second window on the right.

After that, I saw less and less of Reggie, as well as all my other buddies. One night when I was despondent over this, Marilyn, as wives often do, put it all into perspective for me: "They were only your friends when you had some 'get-high.' They were 'get-high' buddies, not friends." She was right, and that reality was so painful. I don't think I've ever gotten over it. Ever since, it's been hard for me to get close to people. The experience with Reggie and the other guys somehow damaged my capacity for friendship.

In my present life, students and colleagues see me as a straight-laced intellectual. If I talk to them about the dangers of drugs, they ask if it's from personal experience. When I tell them I don't drink or take psychoactive substances, they always say, "What about New Year's Eve?" My response is, "Never!" They have no idea who I once was.

You Can't Go Home Again

When my daughters were small, I took them to see my mother in the Lenox Street project. I had a weird feeling about returning and parked close to her apartment building. We walked in a deliberate pace towards 10 Trotter Court, where she lived. Suddenly, I heard a voice, "Hey, Mike." I looked over and saw someone familiar.

When you travel in rough neighborhoods, you have to be more aware of what's going on around you, understanding that at any moment you may become a target. This is a soft learning skill that is difficult to explain, but it may be a survival skill that traces back to the hunter-gatherer society. Or, maybe it's just something you learn from living in the inner city.

We must have been living too long in the suburbs because I was oblivious to his rapid approach until he was too close. Even as he got closer, he looked small but aggressive. I heard a bullshit entry into a conversation, accompanied by a stereotypical light laugh, mandating that I stop. He had all the characteristics of a desperate person, probably an addict. His blue-and-red plaid shirt, jeans and unlaced Timberland boots were oversized and baggy, like hand-me-downs from a larger person. Most telling was the fixed, locked-on gaze of a mugger when his victim is under complete control.

Not being able to return a "Hey, Joey," or "Hey, Mario" made the encounter very tense. We were dressed in our Sunday best, which only made things worse. We kept walking toward the apartment building but were cut off just a few yards from the entrance and I knew what to expect. We'd make some small talk and then I'd be asked for money.

If I had thought ahead, I would have put a couple of dollars in one pocket and the rest of my cash in another, because in this situation pulling out more than a few dollars could result in a robbery. When the "Hey man, can you give me a dollar?" occurred, it was a deliberate ploy to get me to reveal what I had in my pocket.

With all my bravado I said, "Nah, man, I ain't got no money." Then things got really tense. My daughters, seeing another man suddenly approach, clutched my legs, making it hard to move. I was just able to separate a couple of bills from the rest in my pocket just when I heard him say, "If you know what I know you'd give me a dollar!" I gave him whatever was in my hand and we moved on quickly. I never returned there, either dressed up or with my children.

Most of the kids I knew growing up in the projects didn't go too far. A few of them became policemen, firemen and even politicians, but the majority never left. Originally, the projects were supposed to provide temporary housing while you built or re-built your life. But on the rare occasions when I visited my mother, I would see the same people, still there. Often, they would move to another court, or move upstairs, or simply remain in the unit where they had grown up. After that experience, it was clear to me that going back to visit was dangerous. Because I had moved out, I was seen as someone who had escaped or thought of himself as better than the rest. Therefore, I became a victim. I could never go back because I was no longer one of them.

Many times since, I have wondered about the phenomenon of outgrowing your past. On one hand, my socioeconomic origins are so distant from those of my colleagues that I am little more to them than an age peer. At the same time, many of the people I grew up with are no longer my equals in current socioeconomic status. When you look well-fed, well-dressed, and without stress lines etched on your face, are you flaunting your achievements or does it represent some form of personal growth?

Whatever mystique I had acquired from being a rough-and tumble guy from Lenox Street, that phase in my development had ended. At the same time those memories incorporated into my subconscious will always be there, encouraging me to strive for further development. Memories of going to the grocery store with a note asking Mr. Green for necessities until the 1st or 15th when the welfare check arrived still haunt me in my dreams.

All I Saw Was an Angry Man

You will not be punished for your anger, you will be punished by your anger.
— Gautama Siddharta, founder of Buddhism,
563-483 BC

One day, a business appointment caused me to take public transportation into Boston. Since I normally drive, I hadn't been on a bus or subway car in many years. As I rode the escalator down to the lower level platform, I noticed the pigeons and pigeon shit, and the smell of urine from the public restrooms. It made me uncomfortable but the loudspeaker was announcing the departure of an inbound train, so I hurried along, stopping first at a toll booth to buy a card for the turnstile.

I found a spot by the doorway away from everyone else, but riders soon began to invade my space and this also made me uncomfortable. The occasional hacking cough got my attention. The passengers were mostly suburban commuters, traveling to work or school. Some carried cumbersome suitcases, on their way to the airport. They were mostly middle-aged and older white men and women.

The crowd included some bike riders. They were easy to spot by the pants leg stuffed into a sock, water bottle, backpack and other bike riding gear. Most of the commuters slid into the world of their IPods, E-readers, newspapers or text books. I could hear the heavily-accented chatter of some Caribbean commuters, apparently on their way to work or school. This was more comfortable. I had twelve stops to go, so I settled in for the commute.

But when we reached Harvard Square, a major change occurred in the composition of the passengers. The energy level increased dramatically with the addition of a group of loud, rambunctious high school students and a few college-age youths. Although they were just having a good time and doing their thing, one or two were hanging onto the overhead bar very close to me and I became more alert. When we got to the next stop at Central Square, things really changed. The train filled up and I was uneasy with the closeness. There were more young people, more ethnic diversity and a more defined economic stratification. There were more homeless and, most likely, mentally ill riders. A couple were way beyond drunk and years of hard times were evident in their faces and posture.

By now, the demeanor of the young people gave way from commuting students to a more edgy group. The IPod headphones blared gansta rap, full of profanity and racial slurs. The head wraps, tattoos, facial expressions and loud talk impacted me. Suddenly I became self-conscious, wondering how I would handle myself if I were accosted. Although my size should protect me, I'm not as young as I once was. These young guys looked fast and strong. I looked down at all the jewelry I was wearing: two diamond rings, Rolex watch, IPod, Maui Jim sunglasses, gold chain, and a gold bracelet. I'm a walking jewelry store, I thought, and it's all flashy.

The train picked up more students, more teenagers, young and rowdy. I watched the crowd by glancing at people in the reflection of the train's windows. I rolled my rings under so the diamonds didn't show. I pulled my sleeves down over my watch and gold bracelet. I changed my demeanor to communicate, "Don't fuck with me!" I saw my reflection in the train window. On the inside I was nervous in this unfamiliar environment but on the outside, I looked like an angry middle-aged black man.

The subway incident made me wonder if I was an angry person. I thought, why should I be angry? Do I have to have this attitude? Where did it come from? I recognized it as a defensive behavior learned in childhood. In the neighborhoods of my youth, if you didn't look and sound tough, you could be victimized. If you didn't look dangerous, you could be seen as easy prey. In unfamiliar situations, anger can function as a protective shield.

But this defensive posture becomes a habit. Anger is like an addictive drug. Under its intoxicating effects there is an emotional high, followed by a devastating crash. All too often, people would say, "You look so angry" when most of the time, I wasn't angry at all. To avoid seeming angry I began to internalize my feelings but then I would get headaches or stomach ailments. The suppressed anger was making me physically ill. It had become baggage, like a cloak I couldn't throw off. Consequently I became isolated from all but a few people.

Isolation has been a theme in my life. As a light-skinned African-American man, I have experienced both advantages and disadvantages. In the white world I am seen as less threatening than the stereotypical angry black man whereas in the black world I have to repeatedly prove my "blackness." I have to be more assertive, more political and more hip than darker-skinned African-Americans. My wife Marilyn is dark-skinned and I have noticed that many light-skinned black men are drawn to the darkest of women; possibly to compensate for their own light complexions.

As Marilyn and I acquired a more middle-class lifestyle, I discovered that social climbing also has perils. The psychological damage may sting mercilessly, as our experience in the next chapter will demonstrate. The public has become keenly aware of upwardly mobile people in their efforts to make the right impression in attempting to fit in. They may be perceptive of every action, even the intonation of speech and body movements. In response, it is necessary to show patience and consideration. In this social minuet, the slightest deviation from the status quo is noticed and interpreted as another example of the angry black man. This in turn causes anger, and the cycle continues.

As a young man, when I became angry I was out of control. I would say the most insulting things, or impose my will through intimidation and the threat of violence. Needless to say, this behavior was never displayed in professional situations. In my younger days, when work situations made me angry I would remind myself that I was highly qualified and could always get another job. Nevertheless, over the years the angry persona became a burden.

In Buddhist philosophy anger is a condition that resides in the world of Hell, and spirals up and down in a continuum of severity. It is the lowest life condition and represents a state of torment. Ichinen sanzen is a basic Buddhist life philosophy which literally means "3000 realms (sanzen) in a single moment of life (ichinen) experienced by a person's mind. It is an integration of the Ten Worlds, their mutual possession, the ten factors and the three realms of existence, which when multiplied translates into 3000 realms in a single moment.

One does not continually reside in a particular world but rather floats between the Ten Worlds depending upon their circumstances. A person who is normally in a world of Hell may hear a funny joke and laugh, temporarily moving that person into a higher world. Even the angriest person may be momentarily happy and content.

Over time, I have learned another way. I chant in the morning and evening, during which I review areas of potential stress. By viewing them with dispassion, the issues rise to a level at which I can consider them with objectivity. In this manner, I frequently discover alternative ways to solve problems. This makes me feel confident, relaxed and in harmony with my environment. As I subsequently move through the day, I feel able to handle the obstacles before me. This provides a positive reinforcement that causes me to chant more, and in the evening, I chant to give thanks for a successful day.

Through this discipline, my anger has gradually subsided and a new me has emerged. Like conquering some kind of addiction, I have conquered my anger. I have left the world of Hell and now reside at a higher level. My goal has been to have a stable and harmonious life and to simply be happy. Through this process, I have managed to turn the poison of anger into medicine.

Research has shown that the more education you have the less likely you are to go to jail. In that sense, education was my salvation because my background as an inner-city black male would suggest that my chances of being incarcerated were fairly high.

Spiritual education may have the same result. During the 1970s, the Black Muslims were seen as advocates and saviors for turning around the lives of convicts, drug addicts and murderers. These converts were able to find new life direction by embracing the principles and discipline of the Muslim faith, which discipline had most likely been lacking in their upbringing.

Similarly, I discovered from interviewing some local practitioners of Nichiren Buddhism, that in the 1970s, outreach initiatives were undertaken in the drug rehabilitation facilities of Roxbury. I was surprised to learn that as a consequence, some of our most disciplined practitioners owe their current stable, productive lives to those outreach efforts. The initiative was evidently spearheaded by a group of Japanese women, some of whom were the wives of servicemen returning home from military duty in Japan. Those early converts spoke of the discipline inherent in the practice of Nichiren Buddhism as a breakthrough in their struggle to reclaim their lives.

Not Your Average Suburbanite

In the early years of our marriage, Marilyn and I started attending yard sales as a Saturday morning leisure activity. As we scoured the knickknacks laid out on boxes and folding tables, we found many interesting home furnishings that were either unavailable or unaffordable at Filene's and other department stores. Supplemental sets of glasses or cookware, for example, that were luxuries on a tight budget, when purchased for dollar or two provided a low-cost enhancement to the quality of life. Gradually, we became experts at identifying the gems among the discards.

We began looking in the classifieds and mapping out routes to secluded locations. This evolved into going to estate sales to find higher-end items. We began to buy table linens, doilies, paintings and artwork, all acquired at a fraction of the normal selling price. In some cases the sellers were just liquidating the possessions of a deceased parent. Sometimes a widow would be moving in with her children and unable to bring everything she had accumulated.

As our excitement over some of these finds grew into a hobby we started to research value on such items as Rosenthal flatware, leaded crystal, original paintings and sterling silver. I bought a jeweler's owl to be able to better view the engravings and got a copy of Koval's Antiques and other reference books. Eventually, we started going to actual auctions. Bidding was fun, but the competition of outbidding someone and winning the auction was even more exciting. So this became a weekly activity and we spent long hours at auction houses. Sometimes we won things we liked but turned out to have little value; in other cases, we acquired quite expensive estate items for a fraction of the price.

Left: A porcelain compote that was for sale at the auction
Right: A crystal compote that was for sale at the auction

We amassed quite a few signed paintings. Marilyn has degrees in art, so she focused on paintings by noteworthy artists such as those belonging to the Hudson River school. She developed an uncanny ability to identify quality work by obscure artists. I concentrated on plates, glasses and soapstone pieces. We would sometimes find other unusual items that we just couldn't pass up, such as ivory-handled letter openers, magnifying glasses or 19th century black memorabilia, which was then quite sought after. Occasionally, I would find Asian relics to add to my collection of Buddhist artifacts. We also obtained beautiful antique furniture—so many chairs, tables and buffets that there were too many to even give to our children!

By the 1990s the country was in the midst of the housing boom, so Marilyn and I were consequently thinking of doing a home addition. I didn't know anything about real estate equity and was surprised to find out how much we had accrued. I thought you simply paid the mortgage and eventually either owned the house or sold it at a profit. I didn't realize you could leverage this investment but Marilyn did, so we leveraged our properties to build the addition.

The problem, we discovered, was that we had acquired so many antiques, furniture pieces, paintings and the like that if we put them in storage during construction, the cost would have wiped out the initial savings of buying them cheaply. So rather than lose money, we decided to sell some of it to offset the cost. Because we had participated in so many auctions and estate sales, we decided to hold one.

At first, I did not like the idea of opening our home to the public. Even though we had lived there for more than 20 years, I had never felt accepted in the community. Family members had come to parties or to visit and later called us to say the police had followed them to the edge of town. And these were older people, driving luxury cars. When I took my clothes to the drycleaners, the attendant would tell me I could pick them up the next time I was in Lexington, assuming that I didn't live there.

Neighbors' holiday parties were another source of discomfort. Whenever we were invited, I always felt patronized, as if the invitation were more an act of political correctness than a gesture of friendship. After all, it seemed, how would it look not to invite the neighborhood's only black residents? In support of that theory, I once heard the adult child of my Indian neighbors say to her parents, "Didn't you realize they only invited you because you're Indian?"

One time, a misdelivered package caused me to ring my neighbor's doorbell. I had lived next door to these people for at least 10 years, during which they usually smiled politely and waved when I drove by. But when I went to deliver the package, I was stunned by the reception. My neighbor refused to open the screen door and opened the main door only a crack to peek through and ask what I wanted! I left with the feeling that no matter how long I lived there, how well educated I was or in what income bracket, I would never be accepted as anything but a "black neighbor."

Despite my misgivings, we decided to have the estate sale. I posted signs around the neighborhood with maps and directions. We polished the floors, bought juice, grapes, cheese and crackers. We had labeled all of the items with their age, vintage and price. It was a bright sunny day. Our hardwood floors revealed the beauty of oak and wax. The crystal glasses sparkled. Vases and cutlery were displayed on quarter-sawn end tables. There were displays of Irish linen and doilies, along with the many other household items. It was an impressive viewing.

Slowly, people arrived. They came in, looked at the items and frequently remarked that the house looked like a museum, and how beautiful everything was. Then they noticed the prices. Many of them had not understood the difference between an estate sale and a yard sale. When they saw tags with $50, $100 or more they were stunned, and left grumbling.

Gradually, I got the feeling that this had not been such a good idea. More than once I noticed people seeming to spend more time looking at us than at the merchandise. I heard comments like, "Where did you get all this stuff?" I said these were things we had accumulated over the years, not grasping the insinuation. Later, it dawned on me that they were actually saying, "Where did you get all this stuff?"

Since no one was buying, Marilyn decided to go outside and work in the garden, one of her passions. As I looked out the window, watching her in the bright sunlight, I noticed cars slowly driving by, their occupants looking at my dark-skinned wife and driving on. The implications were all too obvious.

The event was a bust. We made $35.00 selling a couple of things to one of my Buddhist neighbors, who probably bought them to be supportive. We had spent more than we made. One of my cousins, who had shown up along with some other relatives to help out, started drinking the juice and eating the grapes, cheese and crackers. I was contemplating how much money I had lost when I heard the blare of sirens.

A police car pulled up to my house and everyone became alarmed. Two potential customers left in a hurry. A young policewoman came to the door and said they had received a call from someone who gave our address, saying, "There are some people selling some pretty high-end stuff and it should be investigated." I was almost too stunned to answer. The policewoman asked what was going on and I said we were in the process of renovating our property and were selling some things to offset the cost of storage. She walked around the living room, looking at items and prices. I began a steady chatter about how we had become collectors, mentioning the Lennox Crystal, pointing out the inscription on the Rosenthal cups and plates, flipping open the Waltham pocket watch. I showed her the ivory-handled letter opener. She was clearly impressed by my knowledge, tone of voice, and informed presentation. Her demeanor changed, and, upon leaving, she actually apologized.

Nevertheless, my family and I had been publicly humiliated and my worst fears had been realized. Even though I will never know who made the call, I will always wonder what would cause someone to perform such a despicable act. In my anger, I reported the incident to the local newspapers. None of them answered my call, nor responded to the message left on their answering machines. Then I reached out to a black-owned inner-city newspaper. To my relief, the phone was answered and I was passed along to a reporter. When I told him my story, he was appalled and asked if he could come to the house for a full interview. I agreed.

He arrived within an hour and we provided him with an emotional account of the events. He took notes, snapped pictures and an article appeared in the newspaper. Soon afterward, Marilyn and I were approached by various acquaintances who saw the story. Some people recounted similar experiences, others questioned how long, how educated and/or how much money one must make in order to be accepted by the wider community. A third group chided us for having the gall to move to an affluent, overwhelmingly white community and expect better treatment!

One evening I was sitting in the living room when the doorbell rang. It was the local chief of police. He asked to come in and sat down. He was exceptionally polite, explaining why a patrol car had been sent to our house, that when such calls are made, they had no choice but to respond. He said that other hate crimes had recently occurred in the neighborhood and in a nearby shopping mall, and that the community had been leafleted with Nazi and Aryan hate group material. The perpetrators would place printed material in a sandwich bag weighted with gravel. During the middle of the night, they would throw these packages onto people's driveways in a selected area. The Jewish families who were the target of such acts would find the package on their way to work in the morning. They were devastated, and said they felt very vulnerable in the community.

The police chief's story reminded me of a time at the mall parking lot when I found a disturbing racist publication on my windshield. I remembered looking around and wondering if my car had been singled out. He invited us to participate in a group that was meeting to share such experiences with other townspeople in the hopes of avoiding future attacks and to reassure the victims that they were not alone.

This whole incident reminded me that persistent stereotypes had a greater impact on some of my neighbors than the occasional portrayal of stable, two-parent, middle-class, educated black households such as those depicted in the "Cosby Show." Even though I have lived in this community for more than 20 years, in most instances beyond the superficial, the stereotypes have prevailed.

PART III

To the extent that we contemplate ourselves and elevate our state of life, we can deepen our understanding of others. Someone who does so is capable of recognizing and treasuring people's individuality. A person of wisdom tries to invigorate others and bring out the best in them.

— Daisaku Ikeda

Churches, Clubs and the "Chitterlin' Circuit"

The Lenox Street Housing Development where I grew up is in Boston's South End district, just a few miles from the coastal bays of the Atlantic Ocean. On misty, drizzly days you can smell the salt from the ocean. Seagulls frequently fly over the projects in search of food. In the 1940s, many first-generation immigrants lived there before moving to the suburbs. Some of the five-story red brick walk-ups still had Portuguese or Armenian grocery stores in the basement, and some of the food and butcher shops that had once served Jewish immigrants were still owned and operated by Jewish shopkeepers. Their new clientele were the latest arrivals of the 1960s: African-Americans. In the 19th and early 20th centuries, Boston's black population had lived on the backside of Beacon Hill but had slowly spread southwest to the South End.

The Lenox Street development covers an area of one square block. I lived near the intersection of Lenox

Street and Shawmut Avenue, a neighborhood that had once been the home of Malcolm X, Khalil Gibran, William Monroe Trotter and Orson Welles. Within two blocks of my bedroom there were several nightclubs, including Big Jim's Shanty, Party Café, The Blue Moon and Basin Street South. These clubs formed the "Chitterlin' Circuit," where black entertainers performed during segregation. Notable performers such as Billy Eckstine or Ike & Tina Turner would play at "The Shanty."

Big Jim's Shanty at the corners of Washington and Northampton Streets, 1978

To the neighborhood boys, it was high excitement to be able to get within touching distance of entertainers such as the young women known as The Supremes. We were so close that as they got out of their limousine to enter Basin Street South, Roosevelt Mouldon, a neighborhood teenager, was able to slap then-lead singer Florence Ballard on her behind. She turned, looked at "Rosey" and smiled.

Louie's Lounge at the corner of Washington and Northampton Streets, 1975

In addition to these "high-end" clubs was a lower, far more dangerous group of venues. The Party Café was in this group, offering free
admission for women wearing the shortest mini- skirt. "Miniskirt
night," "big-leg night" and similar promotions were their standard
practice to bring in customers. Frequently at night I could hear the
sound of gunshots coming from the Northampton-Washington
Street area where these clubs were located.

Even closer to my bedroom window were the neighborhood churches — seven of them within a two-block radius. Three were located at the intersection of Lenox and Shawmut Avenue: New Hope Baptist, a discrete storefront church and Father Devine's Holy Rollers. The fourth corner was occupied by the project's apartments. Further up Lenox Street was St. Augustine's High Episcopal Church and, still further up, was Saint Philip's Catholic Church. The New Hope Baptist and Father Devine's Church held what seemed like a weekly musical competition. Each church had a full complement of instruments: drums, piano, saxophones and guitars. Father Devine's singers were far more mournful and heartfelt than the comparatively refined New Hope choir but both churches raised the roof and spilled out onto the streets with their music. The nameless storefront church could not compete with the powerhouses on the other corners.

St. Augustine's Episcopal Church.
Just off the corner of Lenox Street and Shawmut Ave

I attended various neighborhood churches although I seemed to belong to Saint Philip's Catholic Church. I had been baptized Catholic as an infant, so I thought I had no choice in the matter. When I attended the Protestant churches, I would do inappropriate things, like make the sign of the cross before praying. I enjoyed the Protestant service because it was more invigorating. People moved around, singing at the top of their voices. The minister was lively and his sermon had a message. Most of all, the minister and much of the congregation looked like me.

By comparison, the Catholic mass seemed sterile and bland. The priests were white and wore purple and white robes. The church's vaulted ceilings made the service seem distant, other-worldly. The congregation often did not look like me and sometimes looked at me as if I did not belong there. But the leap from Gregorian chant to the Evangelical congregation, with people talking in voices, was too great so I stayed in the Catholic church. I did not consider the Protestant service appropriate for my worship.

One of three churches on the corner of Lenox and Shawmut Avenues

I was fortunate to attend the Catholic church when it was experiencing a kind of renaissance. St. Philip's had two young priests who reached out to the young people in the community, so a group of us began using the church as a gathering place and met there once a week. Mostly, we just hung out but eventually organized and started giving parties to raise money for out-of-town trips. I was elected president of the group on several occasions, which was the beginning of my experience in leadership roles.

One of three churches on the corner of Lenox and Shawmut Avenues

In spite of the enjoyment in belonging to the group, I was still disenchanted with the Catholic Church. It seemed too bourgeois. I suppose there were congregants from all strata of the community, but they seemed to be mostly remnant white people who had not yet left the neighborhood. The black parishioners were few and seemed out of place, even though they lived in the neighborhood. Walking down the aisle to receive Holy Eucharist from an old white man preaching a sermon on lofty, remote ideals did not penetrate the core of my being. I found the experience lacking.

Some of the church teachings seemed so paradoxical they caused me to take a critical look at what this institution was asking me to accept on faith. One was the notion that Jesus Christ, who was essentially born in Africa, was depicted as a blue-eyed white man. Finally, I thought, "What if I don't accept these beliefs simply on faith?" Having asked that question, I walked out of the church and never returned.

One of three churches on the corner of Lenox and Shawmut Avenues

At first, I embraced atheism and was consumed by the notion that this existence is all there is to life. From that point of view everything made sense. When I look back at all that I was supposed to accept on faith, it seemed silly. When I listened to Christians argue that a man rose from the dead, it seemed preposterous. After a number of years and a great deal of thought, I moderated that belief. I began to accept that some things in this life were beyond my comprehension. Because I acknowledged that I didn't understand all aspects of this existence, I became agnostic. To this day I still have problems with the Christian Bible and its many interpretations.

Help From Strangers and Strange Places

Lost in thought, I was on my way to a union meeting, walking down a Lower Roxbury street where my mother and her siblings had often walked. I imagined them, young and healthy, and now only my mother was still alive. My mother's health was failing and I wanted to finish my doctoral program before she passed. These thoughts caused me so much pain that my back and legs hurt. She was proud of my achievements and in our quiet conversations, her assurance that I was going to do well had helped make it possible. I thought my success might help to ameliorate all the struggles she had endured. Her support had never ceased and I wanted her to see it fulfilled before she passed.

But I was in a quandary. The work was not progressing fast enough. The footsteps of her passing were catching up to my progress and it seemed likely I would not finish in time. This tormented me so much I had been unable to sleep. It was a raw winter day in New England, drizzly and overcast. I was wearing a London Fog overcoat and scarf, a wide-brimmed hat and leather gloves. I was preoccupied with mental calculations: getting the job done, meeting my deadlines. Inside my warm overcoat and other winter attire, I felt protected from the outside world, in my own shell.

Suddenly, I heard a woman's voice. "Hello! How are you? Are you going to the meeting?" Two women were approaching from across the street. "Who are these people," I wondered. "I don't recognize either of them. Why are they talking to me?" As they came nearer, one of them spoke. She was a very attractive middle-aged woman, full-figured, with the features of a mixed-race African/Native

American. Her skin had a reddish undertone, high cheekbones and almond-shaped eyes. Her mouth was filled with pearly white teeth. She said, "You're obviously depressed." I was taken aback. This strange woman had invaded my personal space and was now analyzing me. I said, "Thank you," a code for "go the fuck away," and walked faster.

The union meeting was being held in the sanctuary of an historic old church, its exterior covered with traditional New England clapboard. The union members seated in the pews, as if attending a church service. I took off my hat, unbuttoned my overcoat, stuffed my gloves in my pocket and sat down. The women I had encountered on the street were seated in front of me and the one who had said I looked depressed turned around frequently to talk. I simply wanted to attend the meeting, hear what was being said and leave. I did not want to make a friend or be analyzed. I just wanted to be left alone.

She said with a big smile, "You know, I can help you." I said, "Oh, how is that?" She said she belonged to some group that would enable me to achieve my goals. With great sarcasm I responded, "Will I have to give you some of my hair and fingernail clippings? Will there be bare-breasted women dancing around a fire? How much will I have to pay?" I now think of such comments and wince.

Ordinarily, I would have dismissed her as a crazy person but what she had to say intrigued me. She said this group, called the Landmark Institute, was holding a weekend seminar and it would cost $300. I said, "You ain't never going to get $300 out of me." Surprisingly, she said, "If you come and fully participate I'll pay the $300 myself. If you don't find it worthwhile, you don't have to pay me back. If you do, you pay me back." I was stunned. No one had ever offered me such a confident proposal, so I agreed. I would participate and pay her back if I found it worthwhile.

As planned, I met Abeena at a massive technology building in a high-tech area of Cambridge. We took the elevator to the second floor and were greeted by smiling faces. I filled out some forms with my home phone number and address and we were admitted into a huge convention hall where rows of folding chairs were arranged into blocks of 20 to each row. At the back of the room were tables and support staff and at the front was a large podium with audiovisual equipment. It seemed very well organized and running to a scripted schedule.

Hundreds of people were in attendance, milling around and chatting quietly. I noticed that in the crowd of possibly 750 people, there was only one other black person besides us. The proceedings began exactly on time, with a man in a high-tech headset describing what he called "creating a new paradigm in your life." He spoke on topics such as the things we overlook in our lives, our rationalizations enabling us to live with our shortcoming and the outright lies we tell others. Most unnervingly, he spoke about how people with insight can instantly recognize our lack of authenticity.

I was truly intrigued by his lecture, as it represented a completely new approach to problem solving. He then presented examples and developed scenarios, while the audience engaged in hands-on activities. In the course of that weekend, we sat on metal folding chairs for what must have been a total of 45 hours. At times, my legs hurt and I had to go to the bathroom but could not leave the room because I didn't want to miss anything. Eventually, my backside began to hurt, and I noticed that some people had brought cushions or pillows to sit on. I made a mental note to bring a pillow the next day!

His lecture contained concepts I had never considered, such as my way of dealing with people and how I presented myself to the world. I realized that I had developed some lies, told again and again to the point where they had come to represent the truth. On a pad of paper I jotted down some shortcomings that I had allowed to fester, either through lack of experience, faulty training or the assumption that this was what you did to survive as a black man in society.

The seminar made me realize some things I needed to change, but I was surprised that this kind of self-inquiry was available and no one in my community other than Abeena seemed to be aware of it. To me, the most appealing aspect of the program was in confronting and overcoming the obstacles preventing advancement. I desperately wanted to overcome these obstacles and enthusiastically participated in every aspect of the training. As the weekend drew to a close, Abeena said that this was just the beginning. The next session, which was an application of the theories, was much longer and equally as powerful. Then she said it would cost $1,000. I was stunned. I was already wondering how to repay the $300. How on earth I was going to raise $1,000 to continue?

I told her that the money was a problem and she said other members had made appeals to the group for support to continue the training. She said that at the session's end there would be an opportunity to stand up and ask for support of $1 or $2 donations to continue. I was not happy to hear this because I'm not in the habit of asking strangers for money. Also, as one of only three black people in the room, I now had to ask all the white participants to pay my way.

As the session came to a close, I got increasingly nervous. I was determined to continue the training but what was I going to offer these people to make it worth their while? Suddenly, I had an idea based upon my dissertation: I would say that if they contributed, I would dedicate my life to helping adolescent fathers. When the moment came, I stood up and I asked the crowd for their support. I made the offer and handed the pillowcase to the person next to me. Then I heard a voice behind me say, "I will support this young man!" Immediately, an undercurrent of anger surged in me for being referred to as a "young man," since by this time I was 46 years old. The room went black and I couldn't see anything. Someone took me by the arm and led me down the row to a table where I was told to fill out some enrollment forms.

I said, "So how am I going to pay for this?" Someone said, "This lady is going to pay for you." I said, "When do I have to pay her back?" He said, "You are being sponsored by her." I looked around and saw a stooped old white lady. The blue veins bulged in her hand as she put the $1000 check on the table. I said, "Thank you for helping me. I will keep my word and work with adolescent fathers." She smiled and turned around to leave. A young, handsome muscular blonde man placed a full-length mink coat on her shoulders and they left together. Later I was told that she was a doctor who had once been a welfare recipient and now owned a building with a suite of doctors' offices and liked to sponsor people.

Promise and Disaster

At the annual West Indian Carnival in Dorchester I ran into Eileen, an acquaintance from the Department of Youth Services. She asked what I was doing and, rather than give her the usual polite answer, I said I was trapped in a dead-end job. With the wild background of carnival noise making it hard to hear, she told me about an opening for a student counselor at a local high school. As it turned out, that conversation would change my life. I showed up at the appointed time, interviewed and was hired. My responsibilities included counseling and tutoring struggling students. Apparently, my good work had not gone unnoticed. As it turned out, Livaughn Chapman, who had interviewed me for admission to the University of Massachusetts, was a top-level administrator at English High School and had made some inquiries about my job performance.

In order to work in the school system I needed teaching certification, a basic requirement to become a permanent employee. This required that I obtain an undergraduate degree in an area in which I could get certified to teach. Since my undergraduate major had been psychology, I returned to Bridgewater State College to obtain a Bachelor's degree in English. After that, I completed the course work for a Master's degree in English and a teacher's certification program at Bridgewater State College. This took sixteen classes to complete the necessary work, which I did in the evenings and during summer vacation. The teacher certification part included apprenticeship teaching at my school, so I taught an English course during my regular work day, which I found exciting. Even though much of my education career was in administration, I maintained the practice of teaching at least one course a year.

In my second year at English High School I was offered a teacher's contract. Initially, I worked as a disciplinarian in their Traditional Program. After a couple of years my position was upgraded to that of a Specialist. I was in charge of the day-to-day operations of the 500 student Traditional Program at English High School.

I already had a Master's degree from a small local college that catered to continuing education students. Unfortunately, this turned out to be probably the worst educational decision I ever made. The students and some of the faculty were unacceptably unprepared and unprofessional. I graduated with a Master's in Education but was very unhappy about the whole experience.

As time went on I went back to school at Bridgewater State College. I completed coursework for an undergraduate degree in English. That coursework was followed by the completion of courses to get a second Master's degree in English and a teacher certification in English. The coursework at each level was rigorous and I felt prepared to undertake the responsibilities of a trained teaching professional. The door that had been closed ten years before when I failed to complete my teacher certification had finally re-opened.

One day, I received a letter from someone named Wayne Dudley, whom I did not know. His letter outlined a way in which I could work my way through a doctoral program at the University of Massachusetts Lowell campus. I found it hard to believe, so I threw the letter in the trash. A few months later, I received the same letter and decided to make some inquiries. I still had no idea how Wayne Dudley got my name but the second time, I was prepared and I followed through. Once again, another door had opened and a path to further development had presented itself.

When I started the doctoral program at the University of Massachusetts at Lowell, I already had a full spectrum of respon-sibilities — family, employment and investment property. I was working full time in the Boston Public School system and had a part time evening job. My rental property required attention and I had a young family with all of the responsibilities inherent in raising young children. Many of my activities interrelated with one another. I enjoyed employing the administrative theory I learned in my courses to on-the-job situations. I refined my interpersonal skills as I worked with my graduate school cohort. My cohort was a group of eight graduate students who were advancing their careers by obtaining a doctorate degree. All of the group members were high-level school administrators in various school systems. The group interactions were training for work situations that are a part of school leadership.

But as the semesters followed one another, I began to wear down. After the school day, I would drive from Boston to UMass Lowell via route 3 North. In normal traffic this is a 45-minute trip, but at about 4:00 p.m. it becomes a bumper-to-bumper nightmare. The commute wasn't too bad if I was zipping along, but on the days when I got caught in rush hour traffic, I would often find myself getting drowsy behind the wheel. It was a real struggle to stay awake. I tried everything. I turned off the heat in the winter time and opened the window. I even stuck my head out the window to try to stay alert. I would blast the radio. I would sing out loud. I tried everything I could think of.

I even tried closing one eye to rest it. Then after a brief period of time I would close the other eye. I played this game for a while. Then the unthinkable happened. I was sitting in traffic. It seemed as though I had been stuck there forever and I was falling into drowsiness. Unexpectedly, the traffic started moving but I was so overwhelmingly sleepy I couldn't shake it off. Slowly my head began to bob forward and my eyes shut. For some undetermined amount of time I fell asleep. Suddenly I awoke to the sound of a car horn, blasting in my ear. It was the car next to mine. I woke up, was startled and shocked beyond belief at the realization that I had been driving in my sleep at a fairly high speed. I gasped for air as a result of the shock of waking up so abruptly. I could feel my heart pounding in my chest. But there was no pulling off the road and I continued shaking all the way to school.

Unforseen Changes

One day Nancy, one of my professors in the doctoral program at The University of Massachusetts at Lowell, approached me and a few other students, offering to become our dissertation advisor. This is a faculty member who typically guides the candidate through the dissertation process: developing a research platform, data-gathering methodology and then conducting the research. Later, I realized that Nancy was trying to establish her position at the university and this was one of her strategies.

The subject of my dissertation was adolescent fathers and the impact of unexpected parenthood on their educational performance, a previously neglected area of research. At first, the work went well. I read all of the available research data, developed a sample and conducted the research. I handed in volumes of paper to Nancy, so she could read the work in progress and provide a critique. After a few weeks/months, I began to notice that she looked physically ill and very stressed out. During our meetings she was fidgety and even appeared to be developing shingles, a nervous condition. I worried that she would be unable to handle the amount of work I was turning in because her other advisees also had to have been giving her equally large amounts of material.

Then I began to suspect that Nancy was not reviewing my work very carefully, so to test out my theory, I handed in the same work twice. When I received both batches back, they had noticeably different comments. Now I was really concerned, because it looked like she wasn't even following her own notes. In such a long document, every change creates ripples that subsequently have to be corrected throughout the whole dissertation.

I started worrying about the possibility that I wouldn't even finish the program on time, so I asked some other faculty members and discovered that Nancy had not received tenure. She would not be at the university much longer. Obviously, this blow to her career was the basis of her erratic behavior. A few years later, I learned that she had died.

I looked around the campus for a new dissertation advisor and found a professor named Richard, a "young lion" who had recently been hired at UMass Lowell and was quickly making a name for himself. Our initial meetings were all smiles and handshakes. He reviewed my work, complimented me profusely and assured me that things would move along quickly. I was pleased because, at that point, I was still well ahead of schedule. Then we started working together. At first, Richard's changes were stylistic and superficial, and I assumed he was just giving me the sort of redirection that could be expected from a new advisor. But as the work progressed, I became increasingly concerned over his written comments. He was making more substantive changes and some were threatening the work at its core.

Then he requested that I remove entire sections and I could see my work being undone, piece by piece. Until now, my writing had been judged by Nancy and other faculty members as superior, and my grades were excellent. Now, at this late stage, a serious stumbling block had brought the process to a grinding halt. Additionally, other things in my life were not going well. Between the stress caused by my mother's failing health, the responsibilities of maintaining a job and family life and my lack of progress on the dissertation, the pressure was unbearable. In fact, my youngest son Meikle, Jr. was born during this time and I can hardly remember his early years, I was so consumed with the doctoral program.

Anger began to grow inside of me, and my mind ran through various scenarios. I wondered if he thought I was not capable because I was black. Did this Ivy League graduate feel that a former public school student could not complete a dissertation? Ugly thoughts plagued me as I tried to sleep at night. Was I going to become another "A.B.D." (All But Dissertation) student — someone who had done all of the coursework but couldn't finish his dissertation? My anger started to surface in our meetings and Richard was beginning to get nervous. He would make pleasant comments about my progress and I would respond by saying, "Don't tell me it's going well and then hand it back looking like you bled all over it." Then one snowy, winter day I lashed out at him, grabbed my work and stormed out of his office. Richard was rattled. It was clear to both of us that things were not going well.

I contacted Dorothy, my group leader at the Landmark Institute. A major part of my training there had been in overcoming obstacles, so she created a structure for me to follow. The first task was to list my three most pressing obstacles. Number one was finishing my dissertation. She outlined a series of steps to take to resolve that and the first step was to set up a meeting with Richard. Nervously, I agreed.

One evening a few days later, I called him at home. He answered the phone, which caught me somewhat off guard since I had never before been able to reach him directly. I said I was working with some people to help me resolve our problem and asked if he would agree to participate, suggesting an evening and a time. He said it was a school night but then after a pause, said, "I'll cancel my class and meet with you." I didn't understand what he meant and in such situations, I tend to stop cold, thinking it's better to keep things as they are rather than possibly making it worse. I said, "Never mind, don't worry about it," and hung up. The members of my support group, who had been listening in on our conversation, asked what had happened. I told them and they were furious with me.

Several weeks passed before I met with Richard again. I was sitting in his office, waiting for him to finish a phone call with another student. As I waited, I looked around his office. Suddenly, I realized that until now, I had either been so nervous or so angry I had not noticed the furnishings. Hanging on one wall was a picture of Martin Luther King. I also saw a picture of Mahatma Gandhi, and one of some geese flying in a V-formation, a symbol of shared leadership and support. On his bookshelf was a figurine of elephants, each holding the tail of the one in front of it. Books on Eastern religion, self-help and philosophy were mixed in with the educational texts. This was the office of an enlightened, caring person. How had I missed all this before?

He finished his call and swiveled around in his chair. This short, balding, bearded professor clasped his hands in front of him and said, "Meikle, what was that telephone call about?" I said, "We've been having a rough time, so I asked for advice from this Landmark group I'm involved with. They suggested that I confront you and request a meeting." He said, "So why did you hang up?"

I felt ashamed. "I got nervous because I didn't understand what was going on. I never would have expected you to cancel a class for me. Why would you make such an offer?" He said, "Do you know why I have this beard?" Of course, I said no. While living in California, he told me, he had been in a serious car accident and his face had gone through a windshield. Even after extensive surgery, he had significant scars.

The scars, he said, made him apprehensive when he talked to groups of people and he was so self-conscious he didn't feel that he could continue to work in public. Then he found a group that sounded very much like the Landmark Institute, and through their support, was able to overcome his discomfort. He had agreed to meet with me because it reminded him of his own commitment to overcoming his obstacle.

I felt humbled by his confession and the fact that we shared a common experience. I told him I would do whatever it took to successfully complete my dissertation. After that, my work habits changed dramatically. I would work late into the night and fax my changes to him. Frequently, I would send faxes as late as midnight and receive his corrections as early as 6:00 am the next morning. We went on like this for months. After awhile, my work began to take a different shape.

The truth was that my previous chair had had lower standards, and my new professor had been subtly trying to encourage me to produce a far superior work. When I finally reached the point of defending it to the entire dissertation committee, I was prepared. Some of my fellow students had rather harrowing experiences: one person had a heart attack and died. Another told me he had taken quite a few sedatives beforehand. Still others were required to make significant changes to their work and re-submit it.

My defense took a total of 15 minutes, at least 10 of which were taken up by the committee members kibitzing back and forth. I finally said, "Am I through? Am I now Dr. Paschal?" The committee said yes, and some members went on to say how impressed they were and that I should seek immediate publication!

After all that writing and studying, it turned out that the greatest learning experience during my doctoral program was that sometimes you get the most help from completely unexpected sources. Two complete strangers, Abeena and Richard, had changed the course of my life. I believe this phenomenon prepared me for becoming a Buddhist, because I was open to changes that I could never have foreseen.

Opening of My Eyes

I was standing in the pulpit of Saint Joseph's Church, speaking to a large group on the importance of parents, particularly young parents, taking time to have quiet talks with their children. The message was that all too often, in our hectic lives, the pursuit of making enough money to make ends meet overrides spending quality time with our children.

I spoke softly into the microphone, my voice washing over the people in the pews. Deep within my chest, the rhetoric of the lost art of raising well-grounded children formed, then escaped. Its eloquence was surreal. I paused to gather myself and heard voices saying, "Take your time." I noticed tears falling onto the paper in front of me.

I continued with my brief address. I said how important it was to me to be told about the mysteries of life, how important it was to be told that everyone and particularly friends could not always be trusted; and how important it was to be told to keep my secrets to myself. I spoke these concepts as if they were meant to be contemplated later, to remind parents, young and old, of their impact on their children. It seemed to be my goal; my mission.

When I finished I was weak and trembling. I looked down at the calla lilies, long-stemmed, peach-colored with burnt orange edges laid out on top of a box. I saw the people in front of me weeping, women dressed in dark colors, some with veils, men in dark suits. So many old people. I composed myself and looked down at the mahogany box, my mother's coffin. I must have stood for a moment when I heard my sister say, "She's not in pain anymore, Meik." I found my way out of the pew and took my place on the front bench.

My sisters know me in a way that I don't know myself. I have sat around my kitchen table, listening to them talk about me. Their chiding conversation is always peppered with remarks such as, "He was always Ma's 'special'." They knew something. But in a loving way they also knew my weaknesses and protected me.

I was never told about the late-night emergency trips to the hospital. I was called the next day and told that my mother was in the hospital. I would then go and visit, sit and talk and kiss her forehead. I would stop home and make sure she had everything.

It was only on her last trip to the hospital that I had a conversation with the attending physician who told me my mother had had seven heart attacks! I had no idea you could survive so many assaults. My sisters, like women often do, sheltered me from the reality of impending death. They knew I did not hold up well.

The theater that is funerals followed its usual format. There was singing of spirituals including "His Eye Is on the Sparrow." Surprisingly, there was also a lot of laughter along with the crying. I hugged and greeted family members I had not seen in years. I even hugged uninvited co-workers, who would attend funerals as a way to leave work early.

As we left the church my cousin Yvette was just arriving. This was typical of her, always late. Yvette was the cousin whom you wished was not your cousin. In the cultural parlance, she is "fine" and "thick." Yvette is very fashion conscious and even in funeral attire looked stunning. She showed just enough cleavage and an enticing amount of thigh but tastefully done.

Even in my profound sadness, I enjoyed the long hug I received from her. She held me close and shared her energy with me. Just before things got awkward she whispered, "I need to see you soon. We need to talk." I said "Ok, but you know it's always years before I run into you!" She hustled into the church to pay her last respects.

The grief was unbearable. I had not realized how much I relied upon my mother for, if nothing else, simple conversation. But I was having another problem as well. I must have been going through some kind of mid-life crisis. This is when you realize you're no longer 18, 25 or even just 30. I was now in my late forties. The next milestone was half a century. For someone who never expected to make it out of his 20s, I was getting old. Also, getting married in your early 20s means that in your 40s, you've been married half your life. You no longer have that slim, ripped physique. You can no longer stay up all night and still go to work. The big question is, are you still desirable and if so, how do you know? That last concern is where the real problems of mid-life crisis arise.

The combination of grief and mid-life crisis was overwhelming. I found myself coming home after work and going straight to bed. My youngest daughter would bring meals to me. I found myself having much-too-personal conversations with older women on my job. I felt a heaviness, darkness, weakness. This went on for months and only seemed to be getting worse.

Quite by chance I found myself discussing my life condition with a longtime friend, Livaughn. Unexpectedly, he gave me some advice that was clear and simple: "Nobody goes through what is happening to you alone. When my wife and I divorced after 23 three years I needed help to get through the emotional shock. You're obviously depressed and you need to speak to a therapist." I was surprised at this recommendation, but was open to any advice that would make the pain go away. Livaughn recommended a popular black female therapist.

Seven Rays

I enjoyed therapy. The freedom of being able to talk openly without fear of consequences was liberating, as was the ability to give voice to notions, ideas and feelings that rattled around in my head. At times, I was surprised at some of the things I said because they raised serious questions about where I was going in my life. Now I had someone skilled to help me frame these conversations. My therapist based her approach on the esoteric teachings of Alice Bailey, known as Seven Rays. When I discovered that, I was intrigued and immediately went to a bookstore in Harvard Square, asking if they had books by Alice Bailey. The bookseller said, "Oh sure, lots of stuff," and gave me a brief explanation of Seven Rays. I said, "How come I never heard of any of this before?" It seemed like everyone in my new circle of informants knew about Seven Rays but me.

I eventually bought and read all of the Alice Bailey books they had in stock and was able to talk intelligently about the esoteric aspects of the techniques my therapist was using. In essence, Alice Bailey espouses that all is energy, and that spirit, matter, and the psychic forces are forms of energy. This energy is life itself. From one fundamental energy, divinity, proceed seven rays that underlie and shape the evolution of human life and the entire phenomenal world. On a cosmic level these seven rays of energy are the creative forces of planets and stars. On a microcosmic level they are the creative forces conditioning the physical, psychic, and spiritual constitution of man. By understanding that you are in development as a being and all that happens to you is a part of that development you can better cope with life's challenges. This realization helped in my goal to deal with the pain. I became a participant, not just a recipient, in the therapy.

Then one day it happened. I was cutting through a corner gas station when it was as if someone suddenly at once turned a light on and took a heavy weight off my body. The depression was gone. The sky was blue. The clouds were puffy. Instantly, I felt I was back to being my old self. I guess the chemicals in my head got back into balance. I felt great.

However, now that I was no longer depressed I didn't know what to do with my time. I stopped going to therapy but boy, did I miss those chats! Also, I had nothing to read. I liked going to the creepy bookstore with the weird people looking for books on alien abductions and Wiccan ceremonies. I had exhausted their Alice Bailey section and by this time, the owner knew my reading tastes. He suggested I read *What the Buddha Taught* and I took his advice.

What the Buddha Taught introduced me to the foundations of Buddhism. It covered both Hinayana and Mahayana Buddhist teachings, and was both accessible and intriguing. As I read, I found many insightful sayings — concepts I had already arrived at during the meditations I had on my long jogs through Franklin Park. For example, one of the more engaging sayings that "the wife of a thief is a thief," has stayed with me for years. I have always found the role of the enabler to be fascinating.

My mind was swirling with the newly-found concepts of Seven Rays and now, Buddhism. Then it happened. One damp, drizzly evening, I bumped into Yvette in the Stop and Shop parking lot. It was the right time and place. With people entering and leaving the store, we stood there and talked for hours while the high-intensity parking lot lights bounced off the black asphalt. Their blue and red iridescent halos created an eerie atmosphere.

Yvette talked about her Buddhist practice and I was receptive. I realized that if this conversation had occurred just a couple of weeks earlier, in my depressed state I would have respectfully listened awhile, then gone on with my shopping. However, the timing was right and it did not seem like mere coincidence.

When something is going to become a major part of your life, I believe its manifestation does not emerge all at once. Pieces of it may come to you in an amorphous merging of present and future with no clear distinction. Maybe the emotions come first and you feel the change. Maybe you first experience sensations of color or sound associated with the change. It may be a kind of deja vu or a revelation in a dream. But like waves rippling into your life, this new experience or concept slowly makes its presence known.

One example of this is when you first walk into a house and know that it will become your home — the home in which your children will be born, the rooms you will sit and chat in with family and friends. It is as if you can feel the energy of future ghosts and events yet to come. When Yvette first spoke to me of Buddhism, I felt this new way was going to be a major force in my future. Maybe it had always been there, unrealized, but providing support and gentle guidance, while preparing me for a more fulfilled life.

Alice Bailey

Alice Ann Bailey (June 16, 1880 – December 15, 1949 was a writer and theosophist in what she termed "Ageless Wisdom." This included occult teachings, "esoteric" psychology and healing, astrological and other philosophic and religious themes. She was born Alice LaTrobe Bateman in Manchester, England and moved to the United States in 1907, where she spent most of her life as a writer and teacher. Her works, written between 1919 and 1949, describe a wide-ranging system of esoteric thought covering such topics as how spirituality relates to the solar system, meditation, healing, spiritual psychology, the destiny of nations, and prescriptions for society in general. She described the majority of her work as having been telepathically dictated to her by an Ascended master, initially referred to only as "the Tibetan," or by the initials "D.K.," later identified as Djwal Khul. Her writings were influenced by the works of Madame Blavatsky. Though Bailey's writings differ from Mme. Blavaksy's orthodox Theosophy, they share some common themes. Bailey wrote on religious themes, including Christianity, although her writings are fundamentally different from many aspects of Christianity and of other orthodox religions. Her vision of a unified society includes a global "spirit of religion" that differs from traditional religious forms and includes the concept of the Age of Aquarius. One of her theories encompasses a concept known as "The Seven Rays." She, along with The Church Universal and Triumphant, assign different colors and Masters to each of the seven rays, as follows:

	RAY	COLOR	COSMIC MASTER	RESIDENCE	PLANET RULERS	CHAKRA/GLAND	JEWEL
FIRST RAY	Will / Power	Red	Morya	Darjeeling, India	Pluto/ Vulcan	Vishuddha (5th) Throat/Thyroid	Diamond
SECOND RAY	Love / Wisdom	Indigo	Koot Hoomi	Shigatse, Tibet	Sun/ Jupiter	Sahasrara (7th) Crown/Pineal	Sapphire
THIRD RAY	Active Intelligence	Green	Venetian	Chateau de Liberte, S. France & Temple of the Sun, NY	Earth/ Saturn	Anahata (4th) Heart/Thymus	Emerald
FOURTH RAY	Harmony through conflict	Yellow	Serapis	Luxor, Egypt	Moon/ Mercury	Muladhara (1st) Base/Adrenals	Jasper
FIFTH RAY	Concrete Science	Orange	Hilarion	Island of Crete, Greece	Venus	Ajna (6th) Brow/Pituitary	Topaz
SIXTH RAY	Love / Devotion	Blue	Master Jesus	Mount Lebanon, Lebanon	Mars/ Neptune	Manipura (3rd) Solar Plexus	Ruby
SEVENTH RAY	Ceremonial Order	Violet	St. Germain	Transylvania, Romania	Uranus	Swadisthana (2nd) Sacral/ Gonads	Amethyst

Beginning My Buddhist Practice —My Human Revolution

I was nervous when Yvette picked me up and drove me to my first Buddhist meeting. Previously, I had avoided her many requests to attend. Every time I saw her at the supermarket, she would try to drag me to a meeting. But now, it seemed, the time was right. I had done reading and research into Eastern philosophy and religion. I had participated in some guided meditations. For awhile, I had attended Sada Yoga classes. I was ready to take the plunge.

Although Yvette had briefly described what to expect, going to a stranger's house and being introduced to the whole group had my nerves on edge. I wondered who I would meet, and if there would be any other black people besides me and Yvette?

When I go somewhere for the first time, I like to maintain a low profile. I like to get a sense of the environment. But, this time, I knew that was not going to be the case. I would be asked questions and provided with a lot of information. I hoped it was not going to be high pressure. I did not want to join anything or sign any papers. As it turned out, at the end of the evening the only thing I was asked was if I had any questions.

When we arrived I felt strangely comfortable. The environment emitted warmth and its inhabitants, acceptance. Their faces were smiling, their voices were soft. I was invited in and made to feel at home. I sensed that I was being observed but I looked back. I surveyed the room, noticing a number of pictures of Japanese and Indian people. I saw candles and smelled incense. There were chairs to sit in, large pillows to sit on. There were kneelers for the well-seasoned chanters.

You could hear the chanting from outside the house. A mantra was being repeated over and over, Nam-myoho-renge-kyo, but at that time I didn't know what they were saying. A woman was leading it, seated on a low bench in front of a wooden box about 3 ft. tall, 1½ ft. wide and about 10 in. deep. The other participants faced an ornate wooden box containing a scroll. It was constructed of a dark mahogany, with two doors opening in the center and a small interior light. The scroll was written elegantly in vertical Sanskrit calligraphy.

I later learned that the box, called a Butsudan, houses a replica of the scroll originally written by the 12th century Buddhist monk Nichiren Daishonin, whose teachings are the core of this Buddhist practice. To one side of the Butsudan was a bell on a cushion and on the other side was a green plant. There also appeared to be a number of obviously symbolic items, two golden crane statuettes and a golden vessel, which I later learned held water inside the Butsudan. It was a lot to take in all at once but I had come with the intention of understanding the whole experience.

There was only a small group of three or four people attending, and I was the only man. Yvette and I were the only black people but I felt comfortable. I did not look at the others as much in the context of skin color, but more in how they greeted me. They made me feel welcome and I appreciated it.

I was supported through my first experience with Gongyo. It was quite a challenge. The chanting of Nam-myoho-renge-kyo is obviously from a different language. Additionally, the words of the liturgy were all a mixture of Chinese and Sanskrit. I had to pay attention to the pacing and to the tone. Yvette ran her fingers along the lines so that I kept up with the proceedings. I started. I stopped. I was frustrated. I lost my place. My mind wandered, but I kept at it. At several points, a bell was rung. The vibrations hung in the air for a long time. That got my attention.

At different points we stopped reading the sections of the Lotus Sutra and began chanting. I must say the chanting was very long. So long that it became painful. My back began to hurt. I felt the need to move my legs. Obviously, this practice was not for the fainthearted. But, in the home meetings adjustments are always made to accommodate those new to the practice. I looked at my watch and kept track of the time. We chanted for a full 30 minutes.

It became clear to me that the meeting had a definite structure. Twice-daily practice is called Gongyo, a Japanese word that literally means "assiduous practice." In Nichiren Buddhism this involves sitting in front of the Gohonzon while chanting Nam-myoho-renge-kyo and reciting portions of the Lotus Sutra: Chapter Two entitled "Expedient Means" and Chapter Sixteen, "Life Span." This is the basic practice of Nichiren Buddhism, and is performed in the morning and evening.

The chanting at the beginning was followed by Gongyo, with more chanting afterward. Then followed a discussion designed to help practitioners better understand the Gosho, or body of teachings by Nichiren Daishonin. The discussion was led by a practitioner who had obviously studied it in depth. Afterward, the participants recounted some personal experiences that were based on overcoming obstacles.

I was impressed with the entire proceedings. Not only was it comfortable, it involved the kind of conversation I seldom had in my everyday life. I knew I wanted to stay with this. Once I got the rhythm, I enjoyed the chanting too. I could feel the words resonating in my chest, almost like singing. I could hear variations in the intonations of the other participants. After awhile I felt a kind of calmness. My mind wandered but I continued chanting.

The whole experience reminded me of my long-distance runs, when I was inside my thoughts and it felt comfortable. My hectic workday never provided the time to just sit and think. I also became more aware of my breathing, making sure I took in enough air to be able to chant for a prolonged period of time. I was able to be at ease with myself without distraction. It was just me, chanting, and whatever floated in and out of my consciousness. I felt myself, without any effort, reaching deeper levels of consciousness. Despite my initial discomfort at the length of time involved, I was enjoying this. I decided to stick with it.

District Meetings

From the outside, the district center looked like all the other red brick buildings of Boston's South End. You could walk right by it without noticing that it had a different function. After several more home meetings, I was taken to a monthly district meeting by members who were holding the weekly meetings in the Lexington area. Parking was difficult but we found a spot many blocks away. While walking to the center, I was told to expect a diversity of people, many different languages, some of whom with obvious diversity in income. Gongyo, I was told, would be conducted at a rapid-fire pace.

Once inside, it became apparent that this was a Buddhist cultural center. There was artwork depicting lotus flowers representing Shakyamuni's highest teaching, the Lotus Sutra, wherein he explains that all he had taught previously was provisional. He expounds on having an existence that is essentially eternal, with no beginning or end.

The building contained many small rooms off of a central hallway that, I later learned, were available for small meetings or individual chanting. The downstairs had a large central area in which the monthly meetings were held. I took a good look at some of the people. Some seemed to be financially struggling while others sported mink coats. I noticed a wide ethnic diversity, demonstrated by the number of members speaking in various languages.

When I entered the meeting area, I heard what sounded like one strong voice chanting Nam-myoho-renge-kyo. The participants were chanting in perfect sync. The leader was seated in the front of the room before an enormous Butsudan. The setting was elegant, with greenery, fruit and a huge bell sitting on a tasseled cushion on top of a stand. The furnishings were similar to those of the home meetings, but much larger. The many accents seemed to fade away as everyone worked their way through Gongyo. I detected rises and falls in the pitch and intonation of the various voices that floated about the room, as if everyone were singing. The energy was palpable and the experience was deeply moving.

Despite my enthusiasm for the meetings, beginning my individual practice in earnest was not easy. I found it hard to perfect the chanting while performing Gongyo. Even after many repetitions, I struggled with certain phrases. It was also necessary to make modifications to my life. I adjusted my daily schedule to attend weekly meetings. I accommodated my practice by learning more about the Nichiren approach to Buddhist philosophy. I was not about to embrace such an arduous practice without being certain it was something I really wanted. Although I knew I had to be patient and practice correctly, I wanted results. I was determined to do whatever it took to become a highly-functioning Buddhist with a strong practice.

Then another issue occurred to me. How would my family accept my new-found faith? My family members were and still are hard-core Christians. By contrast, Buddhism is a practice that has no intermediary; there is no deity to resolve your problems. Buddhism is centered within you. This is a far different concept than that understood by practicing Christians.

When they learned of my conversion to Buddhism, many of my family members simply dismissed the notion that I didn't believe in God. I was talked to like a child, told I would find my way back eventually and that God would forgive me. Mostly, I was asked a lot of questions that clearly demonstrated their lack of understanding.

I invited my wife and children to Buddhist meetings. On an individual basis they came, chanted and listened respectfully. I wondered if they just wanted to see what Dad was doing. Later, when my son went off to college, he gave his life to Jesus. I had thought that if anyone in the family would embrace Buddhism, he would have done so. However, he did not.

I set up a Butsudan in my house. At first, Marilyn insisted that I set it up in my office, but that made it awkward to host weekly meetings at my house. I wanted to be fully involved, which meant holding meetings. Eventually, as I grew in my practice, Marilyn and I had an in-depth conversation about it. She acknowledged her appreciation of the positive changes that were occurring in me. I said that, since it was my house also, I wanted my Butsudan in a prominent space and would be hosting regular weekly meetings.

She agreed without hesitation. That surprised me, because it represented an evolution in our lives. We had never before opened our home on a regular basis. We had held parties, but this was different. It was a bold move for me as well, as I have always considered my house to be my sanctuary, a place of last retreat.

When I hosted the first meetings, I was surprised to receive many compliments on the decor. I suspect many of my fellow members had never been in a black person's home and were unaware of a black middle-class lifestyle not depicted on the 6:00 o'clock news. Additionally, my wife's artistic flair evident throughout the house was a new experience for some. Many Hudson River school, Indian and Southeast Asian paintings and statues complemented the Afrocentric artwork. The floors were covered with hand-woven Turkish rugs, acquired over many years. This new fellowship represented a revolution in my life. My solitary existence was being diminished and I now belonged to a larger community that accepted me and enriched me. It was an important step in my human revolution.

Cupcakes

Chanting is like stirring a glass with sediment on the bottom. Sometimes I reach a place that disturbs that sediment—memories I have suppressed for years, that I have avoided and not put in proper perspective. Because I have not evaluated them for their contribution to my development, they haunt me. As my Buddhist practice has evolved, I have been able to improve my focus in life. I know these experiences have a purpose and I am trying to maintain that perspective, but even now at times I slip into melancholy.

When I think about my childhood, I seldom remember much good or happiness. What I remember is asking for credit at the grocery store, or neighborhood fights that resulted in someone being stabbed. What I remember is scarcity and fear. Today I live in an affluent community. My house is comfortable and warm. My children, now grown, had both a mother and a father. They may not have gotten all they wanted but they always got what they needed and eventually, what they wanted. Within my community I established myself as someone to be reckoned with. Consequently, my children were left alone and not bullied in any way. Their childhood was very different from mine.

I have a recurring memory from when I was nine or ten years old and we were living in the Lenox Street project. My bed was beneath the window of a small bedroom. I had put it there because of the project's heating system. During the winter, steam from cast iron radiators supplied heat to the building. The radiators clanked and hissed when the heat was on. During the winter, they clanked all day and night, like a cathedral church bell. The heat was relentless and stifling to the point of requiring that the window be open about a foot, in even in the depths of the frigid New England winters.

One winter morning, I awoke to see snow on the window ledge. It seemed that an enormous amount of snow had fallen. Like all children, I wanted to go outside and play. Although it was still early in the morning, I got dressed and went outside. I remember seeing tracks from those who had already trudged by. Since the snow was nearly up to my knees, I walked inside the footsteps. It was still snowing heavily, and was bitterly cold. Then I spotted the brown grocery bag. Someone had given in to the elements and left it right there in the snow. No one else was around—just me and the bag of groceries. Without hesitation it I picked it up and made my way back home, being careful not to leave a trail.

My mother washing dishes in the 1980s

My mother accepted the bag. She did not lecture me or tell me to return it. Most of all, she did not say that what I had done was wrong. But for the first time, I saw what other people bought at the grocery store. What I remember most was the Hostess cupcakes, chocolate with a white swirl along the top, wrapped in clear cellophane. We never bought such foods on a normal shopping trip. When I made some money shining shoes in downtown Boston or at Revere Beach, I would buy myself a treat. But at home we never had such luxuries. We used Welch's grape jelly jars for glasses, Maloware plates and a fork and spoon. Our meals consisted of a scoop of rice or mashed potatoes with a pat of margarine, peas or corn and a chicken leg or wing. I did not taste gravy or seasoning until my teen years. That day, or possibly the next, I was amazed when I opened my lunch bag at school. My usual lunch was two Welch's grape jelly sandwiches wrapped in wax paper in a brown paper bag with my name written on it. This day I was thrilled to find a package of two chocolate cupcakes as a part of my lunch.

This was not the first time I had taken something that did not belong to me. I would go to the local Salvation Army or Morgan Memorial, put on a pair of shoes or boots and just walk out, leaving my worn-out shoes. Every year I stole winter gloves from Dutton's clothing store on the corner of Washington and Ruggles streets. I don't think I was an accomplished thief; rather, I think many of the clerks realized my situation and just looked the other way.

I generally had only one pair of shoes at a time and I wore those until they had holes in the soles. I put paper or cardboard in the bottom of the shoes when they had holes. When the holes were too big for cardboard I would take the shoes to the cobbler and have them half-soled. I wore these until they disintegrated and could no longer be repaired. I never owned more than two pairs of pants. I bought them from a store on Washington Street that sold irregulars for two or three dollars. These were usually defective in some way — a missed stitch or a mislabeled length. I bought my clothes with money I made cleaning hallways, running errands, selling newspapers or shining shoes. I've been self-sufficient since the age of 12 and always had some kind of job.

Growing up I experienced the pain borne out of scarcity that results from being on welfare. I know my mother had a tough time feeding and protecting us. I once heard a group of guys talking about their experiences in jail. They all laughed about the things that had happened while they were locked up, the good times they had in prison. Growing up with little or nothing, being scared and feeling vulnerable may be similar to survival in prison. When I was a child, I didn't realize how far down the economic ladder we were. I did not know the poverty I was living in. All I knew was the importance my mother placed on a good education because as I later realized, she saw it as a route out of poverty. This was the reason that she insisted we get up in the morning and go to school.

I know we had some good times. I know there was laughter. My childhood was not some Dickensian hell. But when my mind wanders, it's not the enjoyable moments that flood back but the times of fear and scarcity, times when we didn't have enough. Those are the memories that return. Those are the memories that drive me and have shaped the adult that I have grown up to be. When I am chanting, those are the memories that I let float by.

Misinformation

As a child, I lived in an all-black project and attended all-black elementary and middle schools. Then by chance, I was fortunate enough to attend one of Boston's premier exam high schools. Even though it was located in the heart of the black community, it was a predominantly white high school, including the student population, administration, teaching faculty and even the custodial staff.

When I first saw the floral relief lining the school's entranceway, I was awestruck. The first floor's marble columns and statues were overwhelming. My previous schools had nothing to compare with the ornateness of this school and I was quite unprepared for the experience.

I felt like Alice in Wonderland. So many things were new and strange. Then there was the aspect of being the only Negro boy in most of my classes. There were a few other black students attending the school but they were in the vast minority. Frankly, I believe many of them liked the status of being the only black student and thus when there were two of us in a class, that celebrity status was diluted. While several of the black students were from either the Lenox Street or Cathedral projects, others came from inner-city middle-class households. They maintained a polite distance from their project brethren.

Growing up in a segregated community is fertile ground for oppressed people to develop a defensive superiority, and these attitudes consequently become ingrained in the minds of children. We all grow up with stereotypes born out of our community culture, our family stories, and our friends' delusional information. Eventually, we may realize that information is far from reality but how long does it take to undo the stereotypes? How prevalent are they in our everyday thoughts? How do they limit development if acted upon before you realize how flawed they really are?

I shudder when remembering a certain situation that caused me to realize that one of my fundamental stereotypes was flawed. On numerous occasions, I had been told that, "a black boy can beat any white boy!" I went to school bolstered with this delusion, and traveled the school hallways with a swagger born from this security. One day, during the normal hustle and bustle of lining up in the school cafeteria for lunch I decided to "cut" in line. With all the bravado I could muster, I went to the front of the line and elbowed my way between two white schoolmates. I remember telling them to move out of my way in a very assertive manner. No one challenged me and I thought I had been successful.

But then, as I moved through the line and was in this close proximity I realized how big some of these boys were. I was 6 feet tall, but weighed only about 135 pounds. Some of my classmates were physically fit, muscular young men. I could overhear some of their conversations about lifting weights at the YMCA, about playing football, about playing baseball and going out for the school's team. These young men were well-fed and physically fit. I had to question the reality of being able to beat any of them in a fistfight. I realized that this baggage I had carried from home was probably going to get me hurt and humiliated. These boys were strong and fit. My stereotypes were weak and dangerous.

I came from a very poor household. I did not know that at the time but my mother was a single parent raising four children and we survived on a welfare check. When I grew older I got part-time jobs and therefore, always had a small amount of cash. My mother had started to instill her values on us, one of which was that you should contribute to household expenses. At first, I contributed five dollars a week. Later on, as I made a little more money I contributed $10 per week. I paid for my school lunches, my shirts and pants that had to be dry cleaned. Essentially, I have supported myself since about the age of twelve.

When I entered high school I began working in the kitchen of Charlesgate West, a part of the Boston University dormitories. I was working seven days a week after school and all day on weekends. My contributions to the house rose to $20 a week. Then I noticed something odd. A couple times I got sick and didn't go to work. When I therefore didn't have the $20 to contribute to the household, my mother informed me that I owed her $20 and that would have to be made up out of my next paycheck. This struck me as odd. When I later worked in the kitchen of the Peter Bent Brigham hospital, the practice continued. I now realize, however, that my mother was simply desperate for money.

When I got married my mother gave me some advice. She said, "A real man brings his check home, lays it on the table and walks away." So for many years, I did exactly that. When payday came around, I would cash my check, bring the money home and give it all to my wife. Most of the time there was no real problem, but on several occasions I laid my money on the table and came back saying, "Oh, I need five dollars. "My wife said, "What for?" I remember thinking, *This is my money, why do I have to explain why I want a lousy five dollars?* This scenario occurred several times before I began to question the validity of the information I had received from my mother.

Later in life, I realized several things about my mother. First, she was a single parent and for whatever reason, had difficulty maintaining a stable relationship. Therefore, her counsel with regards to a marriage was coming from a person who had not been successful in that area. I needed information about money management and marriage from someone who had been successful in their marriage and managing their money.

Also, I had to face the reality of how poor we really had been. When I reflected on my mother's attitude toward money, it became clearer when framed in the perspective of someone who was desperate. Her reality and relationship with money was born out of its scarcity. My reality was different. Although I've never been flush, I've always had resources. My relationship to money is far different than my mother's. Therefore, it is not realistic to base my handling of finances on information I received—not only from her, but from any of my family members.

After we had been married for some years, I was still relying on Marilyn to handle the family finances. This, I came to realize, was a mistake in terms of my personal development. I was relatively old when I learned how to budget. I was nervous when handling the payment of the many bills that came with our responsibilities and was dependent upon my wife to handle these issues. In my mind, I had developed the story that I was the breadwinner who went out and made the money that kept our household solvent. In that way, I had weakened myself and this weakness was born out of messages from my past. Taking charge of my finances was quite a struggle, and my wife was not willing to give up all the handling of money. In fact, in a very condescending fashion she allowed me to pay only a few minor bills. I paid bills like my car loan and insurance.

Years later, I'm happy to report that I have since mastered the complexities of handling a middle-class household budget. That is not to say that my wife has given over the entire financial reins to me; in fact, she generally doles out specific tasks for me to handle and questions me about the payment of certain bills. I do not know if this is the practice in most households, but it is in mine. Nonetheless, I am pleased that I have grown in relation to my handling of money.

What these incidents have in common is recognizing a fundamental darkness that is a part of my being. Although this darkness has been a part of my life, it is only through awakening to the realization of the delusions and faulty perceptions that I have based aspects of my life upon the fact that I can reduce and ultimately eliminate the delusions and fundamental darkness, thereby fully realizing myself as an enlightened being.

Pain and Suffering

According to Buddhist teachings, our lives are filled with illusions. Each of us has a different perspective that can change at any given moment. Nothing is permanent and everything is in a constant state of change. These tenets have had a vital impact on me as well as on an experience that shaped my life.

Aunt Blanche was my mother's older sister. She was a plump woman who a laughed a lot, despite the fact that she had a facial deformity. It wasn't hideous, but it was noticeable. Perhaps for that reason, she thought she would never marry and as a young woman, had planned to become a nun. She was an accomplished ice skater and had an extensive collection of marbles, won in competitions. Aunt Blanche was a truly unique person.

When I was very young, in one of those moments you never forget, Aunt Blanche told me something in confidence that permanently shaped how I interact with others. In a quiet voice, she said, "We are not ordinary people, we are not common. Always be careful and protect yourself. Never trust strangers." The statement, "always be careful" resonated most profoundly. What did she mean?

Whatever it was, the message seemed to have deep, troubling significance. Ever since, I have been wary, especially around strangers. As I grew older, I understood it to be to be a warning about friends who were not really friends. As a teenager, I was careful not to get involved in controversies that really had nothing to do with me. As a young man I was careful in choosing the women I dated and assessing their motives.

When I later became interested in our family lineage I started to ask questions. I asked about my uncle Sonny, who was killed in the Korean War and whose name I carry. For a long time, one of his army uniforms hung in the closet. I asked about my maternal grandfather who had died many years before I was born. Frequently, the answers were evasive, but I attributed that to generational behavior.

My cousin Barbara, on my father's side of the family, had moved to Boston from Jacksonville, Florida. One day she called me and asked why I wasn't speaking to my father. I said, "Because he wasn't much of a father. We had nothing in common and when I was growing up, he spent no time with me and didn't do any of the things that a father would normally do." The fact is, our conversations consisted of hearing about how much child support he had paid. In every conversation, I could hear it coming: "I paid six dollars a week when the other guys were only paying five." Now that I have a son of my own I, know just how much I missed.

But Barbara had a different view. She said that because my father was getting old, I should be more forgiving and not make the same mistakes he had made. So I agreed to visit him. As usual, he mentioned the child support. I endured this comment, we talked awhile about superficial things and I left. After that, I began to have frequent conversations with Barbara. As youngsters we had gotten along well but had grown apart as adults. She was interesting to me because she provided an avenue into my father's side of the family, which I had known very little about. Most of them were living in Jacksonville, Florida and I had never met them.

Barbara had a house in Jacksonville that she was renovating as a future retirement home. On one of her Boston-Jacksonville trips, she invited me to come along to meet some relatives. The occasion was an annual family reunion. I jumped at the opportunity to go to Florida, although the family reunion was of interest to me. Jacksonville was not very impressive, and seemed to have a high crime rate. The homes, including Barbara's, had a high level of security and were surrounded by high gates with formidable locks. This was uncomfortable, and I felt caged in. However, I did get to meet a number of family members. Much to my surprise, they said they never heard of me and didn't know that my father had any children. They looked me over and said, "Well, he looks like us." That also made me feel somewhat uncomfortable. I took a lot of pictures, got phone numbers and promised to stay in touch.

Shortly after I returned to Boston I went to see my father. I showed him pictures of his younger sister, Sunshine, whom he had not seen in many years, and a video of the family. As we watched it, he made disparaging remarks about each family member. I realized that this man simply wasn't a nice person. Then as I was leaving, he called me over to the chair in which he was sitting. Leaning forward, he whispered some things in my ear that were simply devastating. I couldn't believe that anyone would reveal such information just to be hurtful, although I have since realized that facing death, people can become very bitter and say inappropriate and hurtful things. I left, more shocked than angry, and never returned. I realized that I didn't really know him at all.

The encounter with my father was very painful. My perceptions of many of the people in my life, of whom I had fond memories, had been destroyed in a single conversation. Over the following weeks and months in coming to grips with this, I began to take on a new understanding of my life and fell back upon my Buddhist practice as a source of relief. I chanted for peace of mind, for my father's revelation to become a distant memory. I asked for guidance from more senior practitioners and followed it vigorously. But my life and my memories were forever changed.

It was only when I happened on some Buddhist writings on the topic that I realized I couldn't continue to wallow in my pain. These writings spoke of confronting fear and pain, that only when you face your fears can you understand the cause. Only when you embrace your pain can you come to understand its roots and move beyond it. This is not easy or comfortable to do, but it was worth trying, because things couldn't get much worse. I chanted for long periods of time for the people affected by my father's venom, seeing them from a new perspective. From this perspective I could see their shortcomings, and realized that my memories were only illusions, the memories of a child idealizing the people in his life. From an adult perspective, some of these experiences now had a wider significance. Even though I had not been told the complete truth, I was able to verify most of it, and realized that my father's revelations had nearly made me destroy the love I felt for the people in my life.

As a fundamental part of my Buddhist practice I chant twice a day, morning and evening. Although the disturbing memories continue to flow through my mind, over a period of time those relationships, even with people long dead, have changed. From an adult perspective I have been able to accept them as flawed, as young people who grew up dealing with life as it was presented to them.

From this perspective, I realized that in some ways I had misinterpreted Aunt Blanche's warning. In this world of illusions and attachments, I had mistaken where the danger actually lay. I had been afraid of being beaten up or bullied by strangers whereas in fact my greatest pain had come from those closest to me. When I finally realized my attachment to memories of flawed people whom I had idealized, the pain diminished and I released my attachment to those new memories. I have recast words of protection given to me many years ago. Now as I chant, study and strive to reveal my Buddha nature I am more at ease with myself. In an unexpected way I have gained a greater understanding of who I am in this world.

Brother Crow

One afternoon shortly after my mother's death I went for a run in Franklin Park. It was warm and sunny and the park was bustling with activity. A school baseball game was being played. Groups of two or three women were walking briskly in colorful nylon exercise outfits, throwing their arms out before them. I parked opposite the tennis courts as usual, taking a moment to watch the matches in progress. I never learned to play tennis, so the game intrigues me. Some solitary joggers passed, their light sweat and heavy breathing revealing they had already completed the 2½-mile track at least once before passing this spot.

I did my warm-up routine: leg lifts followed by sitting on the ground and reaching for my toes. I stretched from side to side. This was followed by about 25 jumping jacks. After completing 25 pushups I am ready for my run. One last check of my sneaker lacings and I'm off.

This portion of my run skirts a picnic area on the right. There is a slight rolling of the path that prepares me for the upcoming steep incline. On my left is a tunnel, which is why the incline is aptly named "dead man's curve." Many youngsters have crashed their bicycles in the tunnel wall after reaching breakneck speeds coming down the winding pathway.

My goal is always to get this challenging segment of my run out of the way as early as possible. I challenge myself to complete it as quickly and powerfully as I can. As a result of this challenge I am usually exhausted, breathing heavy but exhilarated when I reach the flattened-out top of the curve.

My jogging path at Franklin Park

Just a little beyond was the spot at which I had my initial epiphany. Each time I pass there I remember it as clearly as if it had just occurred. But on this occasion I simply gather myself, catch a second wind and run on. I feel strong, having completed the hardest part of the course. Deep within me, I feel rhythmic breathing and a consistent stride. I am alive and in tune with my body.

This part of the course is about a mile long and flat. This is where I practice my stride. There is a two-lane street on my left. The Franklin Park golf course is on my right. Since my family members have occasionally seen me running my course while driving along this street, I don't want to look like an old man, lumbering along trying to keep up and trying to finish. I stand up straight and imagine myself as a galloping horse plowing down the lane as powerfully and quickly as possible. Often as I suck in air, I scream.

Sometimes I sing the theme from *Rocky III*, "The Eye of the Tiger." With all these antics, I wonder what I must look like.

I run flat out for the last 50 yards of this part of the course. Then I slow down, getting my breath to move to another segment of the course. My run takes me along a winding route past the golf house. There is a gradual incline in the path as I near the golf house. I have never been in the golf house, but as I run past I can see that golfers can buy their supplies and have lunch and drinks there.

To the left is a parking lot shaded by tall trees. At all hours of the day, there are numerous cars parked there. Groups of men and a few women seem to spend long hours sitting in their cars. It is somewhat secluded and private. From snatches of conversations I hear while running by, the regulars are of Southern origin. This entire area seems to move at a slower pace. People grab a beer from coolers in the trunk of their cars. They sit and drink all day and long into the evening. Some are drinking whiskey from the bottle. In addition to being a meeting place for the "boys" to hang out and drink, this is also a place for middle-aged lovers to meet and sit in a car together.

I always take notice of what is going on in this area as I jog through. There is a decline and bend in the path that leads me into a rather secluded section of the park. The trail is littered with broken tarmac, with exposed tree roots that can easily cause you to stumble. It is probably no more than 75 feet from the intersection of Blue Hill Ave. and American Legion Highway — a densely-populated, heavily-traveled area, but because of the trees it seems very isolated.

There are benches here on which I have occasionally seen guarded drug transactions take place. I make certain my gaze does not linger on the young men and women wearing the customary hoodies and baggy pants. With the drugs come criminals, so I am on high alert as I pass through this area and am careful to watch my footing. The last thing I want is to trip or stumble and look vulnerable. Amidst the benches and the overgrown bushes and trees there is a clearing in the canopy of no more than twenty feet, perhaps as little as ten feet. The sunlight streams through an otherwise dim area.

This time, as I plowed through my run nearing the final segment, I turned to my right. In the clearing, swooping down and coming directly towards me, was a large crow. First I noticed that the wing span on this bird seemed immense. Its black feathers appeared to sparkle, reflecting the sunlight as it dove towards me. His body was sleek and small but his head was most impressive. He had a black dagger-like beak set prominently before a smoothly-feathered head. Two deep black shiny unblinking marble eyes on either side of his head captured my eyes. He was beautiful variations of blackness and aerodynamic grace.

He dove straight towards me, coming within three feet. He opened his mouth wide enough that I could clearly see all the way down its throat. I was amazed at how clearly I saw the creature's pinkish tongue. As he opened his mouth I saw his long tongue with a cleft and light coat of white.

The bird talked to me with a resounding, single "CAW!" Then it veered upwards, never frightening me. I knew I had received a message but what was the message? Should I try to rationalize the experience or accept it and let the answer come to me in due time? I desperately wanted to process this information but didn't know how. Maybe I could tell myself this was just a coincidence and relegate it to just one of those things that happens in a park. Or maybe I could sit with the experience and in due time, gain understanding. I continued on my jog but it was unlike any other day. That experience set into motion questions about how our environment, the greater universe or whatever one calls it, communicates with us.

The Buddha

The Buddha's birth name was Gautma Siddhartha, which means "he who fulfills his purpose." He is also referred to as Shakyamuni ("sage of the Shakyas"). As a practitioner of Nichiren Buddhism I have read many books, pamphlets, journal articles, excerpts and other material about the Buddha. Upon research, it became clear to me that his history has suffered the distortion of embellishment. Shakyamuni was a real man who lived, married, fathered and died. Only the most significant aspects of his contributions to society seem to have escaped the poet's touch.

His reputed date of birth varies from 623 B.C. to 403 B.C., although it seems certain that he died at the age of 80 from eating spoiled food. He was born in Limbini, a town either located in present-day India or Nepal, a point still under debate. His father Suddhodhana was married to two sisters, Mahaprajaptai and Maya; Shakyamuni's mother was about 40 when he was born. As was the custom, she was traveling to her parents' home when the group stopped at Limbini; apparently so that she could bathe. While bathing she gave birth. There is a question as to whether she died shortly after giving birth, and her younger sister Mahaprajaptai actually raised him.

Shakyamuni's father Suddhodhana was a member of the Shakyas clan who were part of a larger group known as Kshatriyas ("those who owned a farm"). Suddhodhana could be best described as the chief of a tribe rather than a king. During the time of Shakyamuni's birth, sixth century B.C., the forests had been cleared and this area was transforming into a civilization. However, the world that Shakyamuni was born into was far from that of a Raja. He lived in what could best be described as a compound with mud walls surrounded by a moat. All of the important businesses, shops and artisans were located within the compound. Although, they lived in comfort and had stature, this was still sixth-century India or Nepal and far away from anything resembling a great seat of power.

Shakyamuni was reportedly a delicate child who never left the family compound. Sheltered from the realities of the outside world, he lived a pampered life inside its walls. At 29, he married a woman named Yashodhara and soon afterwards became the father of a son named Rahula.

The legend of how Shakyamuni came to renounce his entitled life begins with his venturing into the outside world. He apparently made a series of trips outside of the compound and each time, was confronted with people suffering life's hardships, including aging, disease and death. The shock of real-world experience was the basis of his decision to renounce his birth status and enter the world as a "seeker of wisdom."

Shakyamuni became a sramana, or homeless person. This was part of a then-current popular movement, the basis of which was to renounce your past life and remake yourself. For a time, Shakyamuni lived in the forest, coming into town to beg for food as was the custom of the sramana.

He wandered for years, interacting with several of the most skilled gurus of the time. Eventually, he found the teaching of each guru to be either superficial or flawed, but developed insight and under-standing as the result of each experience. At one point he decided to become an ascetic, the practice of which is to live a very austere life. After that, Shakyamuni lived in the forest and ate so little that he nearly starved to death.

One of Shakyamuni's teachers taught him to meditate. When employing the ascetic mindset he meditated in the extreme. While meditating under a fig tree, Shakyamuni achieved enlightenment, and he conceived the Four Noble Truths.

The Four Noble Truths

- All existence is suffering

- Suffering is caused by selfish craving

- Eradication of selfish craving brings about the cessation of suffering and enables one to attain nirvana

- There is a path by which this eradication can be achieved, namely, the discipline of the eightfold path. The eightfold path consists of:
  - right views
  - right thinking
  - right speech
  - right action
  - right way of life
  - right endeavor
  - right mindfulness
  - right mediation

As a result of Shakyamuni's enlightenment, he felt freed from the ordinary human condition. Moreover, unlike other sages and gurus of his time, he professed that the truth he had discovered was available to anyone willing to follow his example. According to Shakyamuni, the key to achieving freedom from suffering was to practice his approach to meditation, which focused on controlling the fearful nature of one's mind.

Shakyamuni's experience impressed me. He was trying to make sense of it all, like many of us who are trying to understand this complex existence. Late in life, he reached a critical point and set out to find answers to troublesome questions. It appears, that like so many of us, he did not have a fixed plan. He spent time with several spiritual leaders whom he believed would lead him to the answers. Disillusioned, he left each one, but each time he left he had gained a little and grown more.

He found a group of like-minded seekers and wandered with them, embracing the aesthetic lifestyle and continuing to look for answers. He had a life-threatening experience. Shakyamuni had been engaged in an aesthetic practice that included long periods of depravation including extended periods of fasting. He had grown extremely thin and frail. One day while bathing in a stream he collapsed and nearly drowned. As a result of that incident, he began to reconsider his past. Ultimately, Shakyamuni reached a profound understanding of the complexities of life that he provided to the people of his time and which came to be known as the foundations of Buddhism. He continues to be followed in current Buddhist practice.

Actual Proof

Most people who come to Buddhism are seeking escape or relief from some problem in their lives. A friend or even a chance encounter may bring them to it. They hear you can chant for anything, and that no prayer goes unanswered. Most frequently, they chant for relief from an immediate problem. Most frequently, they get relief in some form. They see" Actual Proof" that this practice works.

Many newcomers to Buddhist practice have a "new practitioner" experience. They chant arduously for conspicuous things, focusing on getting a car, money, and job. Although these goals may at first sound frivolous, a deeper investigation reveals that they satisfy the need to fulfill deficiencies. A practitioner, plagued by the constant of being able to keep the lights on or making enough money to live decently, needs to establish a solid foundation in his/her life. The demographics of the Buddhist community are similar in most respects to the greater community. It seems those practitioners with less education, new arrivals to this country, people with family issues, at least initially chant for conspicuous things

Initially, I chanted for inconspicuous things such as peace of mind and relief from my demons. I learned more about the practice from attending weekly meetings and lectures, I heard testimonials from practitioners chanting about conspicuous things; albeit practical things like not losing their home or finding a job, it was still chanting for things. So I began chanting for things. I used higher-level phrasing in my mind, such as financial security, reliable transportation, but it was still things. Indeed, my financial security improved and I got a better car.

As is the pattern in my life I received a message that rose above the chatter of mindless conversation. I heard this message and it has resonated in my practice. The message was, "Chant larger". Chant as arduously as you can for enlightenment, to be the Buddha and all of the other things will fall into place.

I think it is appropriate to chant for those things that you need immediately to better your life, the conspicuous. But, it is the inconspicuous things that will move us to Buddhahood and ultimate relief from this world of pain and suffering.

It seems that people new to the practice most often need relief from something. Most often, they chant vigorously, with urgency and realize that relief. This is followed by chanting for additional conspicuous things. At weekly meetings, people report breakthroughs that have enabled them to overcome some conspicuous obstacle. However, much less often you hear someone say, "I have recognized a calmness of peace of mind in myself. This calmness has permeated my household. There is a new tone in my life." This is the inconspicuous benefit of Buddhist practice and it is the far greater benefit.

It seems that after the initial introduction to this practice, after learning most likely from reading about the deeper understandings of this practice you do access its less conspicuous and more powerful essence.

However, many practitioners are satisfied with the readings required to be a part of the weekly conversation about a topic being addressed. Our Buddhist population mirrors the greater community who read seldom or only when required. I noticed that when I began mentioning the books that I read about Buddhism only a few members of my group responded. Upon engaging those few in conversation about the subtleties of this practice; the conversations got really interesting. These conversations led to more readings and ultimately a clearer, deeper understanding of this practice, which has fundamentally changed my approach.

But does this suggest some sort of hierarchy? Some sought of schism in the knowledge base. Or is this just a fact of life present in any philosophical, theoretical practice. This Buddhism has been researched and studied for thousands of years by people who have devoted their entire lives to this study and they have begun their study standing on the shoulders of others who based their entire lives on the studies. Thus, we encounter the dilemma that faced Shakyamuni, the historical Buddha. He had to contend with presenting his sutras, his message, to a diverse population of listeners who came with varying degrees of comprehension based upon their education. He addressed nobles, gurus, peasants and farmers at the same time.

Therefore, should we condemn as being shallow or self-centered those of us who practice this Buddhism but are not steeped in intense readings of the many volumes that explain the esoteric and or philosophical subtleties of this practice? Is it fair to make disparaging comments about practitioners who chant for things they need to function in this world of pain and suffering? Or is the shallowness in those commenters not understanding of the realities of the practioner's conditions. Should one who is not dealing with such pressing issues make light of those who have urgent demands staring them in the face every day?

I am by nature a nervous type of person, someone who imagines that tragedy is always a step away and the possibility always exists of falling to the bottom. Through Buddhism, I have come to believe that as long as I am strong in my practice, I can withstand any adversity. This principle is known as having a "strong life condition." Chanting, studying and maintaining faith are the essence of having a strong life condition. But I'm not always that consistent. I would like to say that I get up every day and chant for long periods of time, or that I chant every morning when I wake and every evening before I go to bed, but I don't. Sometimes my practice is less intense than it should be and my life condition is not as strong as I want.

A founding tenet of Nichiren Buddhism is "actual proof," when the practitioner sees results from his/her practice. Along with studying for comprehension, chanting for consciousness raising and having faith in the practice, it is extremely validating to see actual proof. The following experiences demonstrated to me that this practice actually works.

During the late 1980s, in a move to advance my career as an educator, I began applying for higher-level jobs. I sent out so many applications for principal, assistant principal and other administrative jobs that I started to wonder what was really going on in the school system that so many of these positions were available. Occasionally, I would get an interview and after the interview, always got called back. I would always make it to the top two finalists but was never the person who got the job. I started to feel as if some kind of game was being played. Were these jobs really available? Were they only posted to fulfill some legal requirement and I really never had a chance?

After doing some research, I discovered that in nearly all of these jobs, the position was already filled. Many of the administrators had held the job for years and were doing excellent work, but in order to achieve permanent status, the job had to be posted. Consequently, any outside person interviewing for the position really had no chance of getting it. The only reason to play this game was that if you really had meaningful skills, eventually you would get a job. The question was how long that might take.

Finally, my turn came. I interviewed for the job of Director of Curriculum and Instruction at two different high schools. During the interviews, I was relaxed. I had been through this so many times I knew how to direct the conversation. I talked about my dreams and visions as an educator, bringing up topics that were not on the list of questions. I was subtle and eloquent. We shook hands and I left.

A couple of days later, the phone rang and I was informed that I had been selected for both positions. I was elated. For the first time, I was in the position of choosing which job I wanted. One school was in the downtown area, so there was no parking. Prostitutes worked the streets in front of the school even during the day. Evidence of their trade was scattered in the school doorways and throughout the schoolyard. The atmosphere was dismal.

The school I chose was in a neighborhood that had parking, but was in an area that had suffered terribly from desegregation. The Ku Klux Klan had conducted an intense recruitment campaign in the neighborhood, and swastikas and racial slurs were still visible in the playground and on walls near the bus stops. The white families had fled and were replaced primarily by black families from the Caribbean.

The school was in disarray. It had been completely neglected during the years of desegregation. The teaching staff was in shambles. The older white teachers were in a state of shock. The white students whom they had taught for years were gone; replaced not only by black faces but worse, West Indians and Haitians of dubious citizenship. The principal who oversaw the transition from white to black and Caribbean had allowed this situation to fester so a new principal had been hired to clean up the mess. The new principal had worked hard and made some improvements, but when I arrived the school was still in terrible shape.

I was ecstatic. I had a disaster to fix. Furthermore, in the principal I had a capable leader to work with and learn from. Students' test scores were horrible, discipline was out of control, teachers were not being held accountable, and staff and student absenteeism was far above the norm. This was a new administrator's dream because there was nowhere to go but up. Any initiative I took could only improve the school's current condition.

For nearly five years, I was able to achieve good results. Test scores were going up, teachers were writing lesson plans and discipline was getting under control. Then the reality of urban schools and local politics reared its ugly head. The superintendent, possibly under pressure from local elected officials, suddenly began to blame the headmaster for conditions that were actually caused by the previous headmaster's neglect. Soon after, it became clear that the headmaster was on his way out. Summer vacation came and the principal who had hired me was demoted and moved to another school.

As often is the case, the new headmaster was anointed as a "change agent," meaning hatchet man. His assignment was to "clean up the place," code words for "get rid of the staff." However, since in the school system one must receive a series of unsatisfactory evaluations to be terminated, this seldom happens. So the staff was simply pressured to transfer to another school or retire.

The school's administrators were forced out in various ways. My position as Director of Curriculum and Instruction was simply written out of the budget. I was stunned but not surprised. It was hard to control my emotions, because I had not done anything wrong. The initiatives I had enacted had been successful. But the headmaster wanted to handpick a new administrative team, and I was part of the old team.

Koi Pond

All of this occurred just before school vacation, when my family was anticipating the carefree days of summer. Suddenly, I was looking for a new job. My wife and children knew about the situation and expected I would be stressed, upset, irritable, depressed and above all, angry. They were looking forward to going to the beach, not functioning on high alert because Dad was out of control. It was not fair for me to deprive them of time off from school, the rest and enjoyment of summer.

Every time I thought about having to interview for a new job, I got angry. I knew how counterproductive this was but periodically, I would slip into a rage that permeated the house. I needed a distraction, something to occupy my mind. I worked on my resume and applied for jobs. I had too much unoccupied time and the problem was, when my mind wandered I got upset.

I needed a place where I could sit and chant, a quiet place, possibly with water. Using part of my back yard, I decided to create a Koi pond with a waterfall. I got some library books on creating the pond and searched Amazon for books on building a drywall. Building the Koi pond kept me busy, although occasionally my thoughts would wander and I would still get upset.

Whenever I started to get angry I would sit before my Gohonzon and chant until the anger subsided. Up to this point, my practice had been confined to chanting morning and evening. Chanting as an antidote to anger and anxiety was new, and I found myself chanting for long stretches of time.

At first, I chanted to move my thoughts away from the anger. But after awhile, I realized my thoughts were beginning to move towards finding solutions as I started to see things from different points of view. I started visualizing myself in a new job, not just any job but one that I really wanted.

Gradually the Koi pond began to take shape. I located some cobblestones in a nearby quarry. I would go to the quarry in the morning, pick up as many stones as I could fit in my SUV and come home to work on the pond. I would chant when my mind wandered. My family was not obliged to suffer through their summer vacation—I was under control. Nevertheless, time was passing and I was not getting any phone calls for interviews. I had mailed approximately twenty-five resumes for jobs that I felt qualified to fill. Working on the pond and chanting was helping but summer vacation eventually ends.

As August arrived the pressure began to build. I worked, I chanted and I visualized. Sometimes I would slip into moments of depression but when I chanted I always managed to maintain faith that this was going to work. In a conversation with a colleague about not getting any response, she said, "Why don't you call or stop by every school you applied to?"

At first I dismissed the idea but the words stayed with me. Later, I was chanting when the concept of visiting schools or calling headmasters came into my consciousness. I was intrigued by the idea of doing things in a different way, and that became a motivating factor. It felt good to move from a passive position to being actively involved in making things happen.

I called the schools but the headmasters were too busy to come to the phone. I drove to the schools, but they were in endless meetings, preparing for the upcoming school year. Their secretaries assured me they had my resume and would call me. More than once, I got the feeling I had been blown off. Calling the schools and interacting with the secretaries in a constructive way became part of my daily routine. Still, I was running out of time.

My original koi pond

In early September I called a middle school that was low on my list of preferred placements. By this time, I was adept at interacting with secretaries and asked if my resume had been received and if the assistant principal position was still open. The secretary said yes and asked if anyone had contacted me. I said no. She took my resume to the headmaster and returned shortly thereafter, asking if I could come to the school for an interview. I said yes.

The headmaster wanted me to be there in an hour. I requested it be expanded to two, allowing me some time to clean up from doing yard work and to briefly chant for the interview's success.

I chanted all the way to the school and it calmed me. Instead of playing my usual radio station, I switched to the classical music station. I wanted to maintain the idea of doing things differently.

At first, it went smoothly. After so many interviews, I had learned how to insert a mention of my skills into the conversation and how to direct the questions in a way that allowed me to outline my accomplishments. Then disaster struck. The headmaster asked what was obviously a key question, pivotal to the success of the interview. He said, "If you're so good, why hasn't anybody hired you? Somewhere deep inside of me, the anger woke up. I had chanted for so many hours. I had controlled the anger and relegated it to a lower world within my being but at this critical moment, here it was. Then I realized that here was yet another opportunity to take a different path. I could have been my usual sarcastic self. I could have lashed out in a long rant on school politics or other self-defeating responses. Instead, in a new way for me I said, "I don't know."

When I left the building I called my former headmaster to alert him that he would be receiving a phone call. I said his response would mean the difference between me getting the job or not. He said he understood. Even before I got home, Marilyn called to tell me I had been offered the job, three days before the first day of school.

My Koi pond is now a place for quiet reflection and deep thought. My wife thanked me for being under control and not wrecking the family's summer vacation. I gained tremendous insight and actual proof of the power of chanting Nam-myoho–renge-kyo.

The Middle Way

During the social turmoil of the 1960s Boston was a city in transition. The African-American population that had been previously relegated to the South End began to expand, partly as the result of the influx of blacks from the southern states and the West Indies. Residents began moving southward into Dorchester, Roxbury and Mattapan. Some of these areas, such as Roxbury's Blue Hill Avenue, were formerly home to Boston's Jewish population, which subsequently fled the influx of African-American homebuyers.

Area real estate agents pounced on the opportunity to make a profit through what is now called "block busting." Fearful of a decline in property values, some of the Jewish homeowners sold hastily, at far below market rate. But block busting didn't stop there. A black middle class was now emerging in Boston, a group of well-educated, upper-income people. They had taken advantage of newly opened doors in the marketplace. Boston had also experienced a growing population of African-American civil servants—policemen, firefighters, teachers and insurance agents.

The formerly Jewish section located along Blue Hill Avenue was still the inner city and this new African-American middle class yearned for suburban life. So they moved even further south and southeast, into the Mattapan and the Hyde Park neighborhoods of Boston. Although this district is part of the City of Boston and therefore not technically the suburbs, it contains many one- and two-family homes and has a distinct sense of community. African-American homebuyers were restricted by strangely high property prices from moving into truly suburban housing, such as those located in West Roxbury and Milton.

Once again, area real estate agents frightened homeowners with the prospect of property devaluation as the African-American families began to move in. Once again, homeowners rushed to sell their homes far below market value, moving further out into the suburbs. Frequently, the new arrivals were better educated and made more money than the former occupants, but the longtime residents who stayed in the neighborhoods nonetheless felt superior. The transition was fraught with peril, with highly-charged confrontations between new and long-time community residents. Local parks had been divided into control areas, the basketball court for the blacks, and the hockey rink for the whites. Neighborhood schools were the scene of numerous racially-motivated fights. It took many years for things to settle down.

When we were first married, Marilyn and I lived in a series of apartments. Initially, they were modest because it was what we could afford at the time. A few years later, we moved into more upscale apartments and finally landed in a pseudo-gated community with various luxuries, but very expensive.

Then Marilyn discovered an opportunity to buy a two-family house in Hyde Park, a nice, safe neighborhood. I was amazed that we could live in our own two-family home for a fraction of what we were then paying for our apartment. I remember the realtor who sold us the house saying, "Now you can buy a Cadillac."

Things were good in Hyde Park for many years. Eventually, however, the complications of raising children in a two-income household became apparent. Many things could happen in the four-hour time span between children getting out of school and parents coming home from work. Some of the neighbors' children had lucrative allowances and access to their parents' cars.

At the same time, we noticed a steady decline in the neighborhood. City services fell off. Requests for liquor store licenses became a problem. The neighborhood children grew older and teenage pregnancy became an issue. Drug dealers and other predators crept into the neighborhood, taking advantage of the lucrative allowances given to neighborhood teens. A surge in home break-ins indicated that drug abuse had reached epic proportions. The once idyllic neighborhood had become a victim of urban decay.

Once again, my wife decided it was time to move and inquired about real estate in Randolph, on the other side of the Blue Hills mountain range. A well-intended friend had told her that Randolph was an up-and-coming suburban town. It had been a Jewish stronghold, so the familiar cycle began again. African-Americans with enough income were fleeing Mattapan and Hyde Park to Randolph. Our children were participating in the M. E. T. C.O. voluntary busing initiative and were attending school in the prestigious Lexington public school system.

It was easy to find a realtor. They had seen the flight from Mattapan and Hyde Park and were well positioned to take advantage of an influx of middle-class African-Americans. We bought a huge two-family home in Randolph but too late, discovered that among other things the Randolph school system was in a sharp decline. We could not take our children out of the prestigious school system in Lexington and enroll them in an inferior system such as the Randolph public schools. We were stuck.

We now had two houses. We had bought the two-family house in Hyde Park, so I knew the challenges of being a landlord. But the idea of owning two houses was attractive. Home ownership had always been a secure investment. Maybe this wasn't so bad after all.

Collecting rent and maintaining the property was a headache. I had been run around by one of our renters in the Hyde Park property. When things went well, the rent was paid on time. Other times it was a nightmare. One way of avoiding this problem was to rent to low-income Section 8 tenants because the government paid most of the rent. These tenants theoretically wanted to maintain their Section 8 and paid their portion of the rent. This seems easy enough. The only complication was the annual Section 8 inspections.

In the Hyde Park house, the Section 8 inspections were simple enough. The inspector came in, marveled at the apartment and we passed almost automatically. Initially it was the same with the Randolph property. Inspectors would marvel at the apartment and say, "I wish I lived here." It was so much easier than chasing tenants for back rent.

Then things changed. Section 8 inspections became more difficult to pass. It was nearly impossible to pass the first time, so failing inspections became routine. This was scary because you could have tenants living on the property and not paying rent and you had no recourse because you couldn't evict them. Inspectors became increasingly demanding and would fail properties for minor infractions.

Eventually, a number of circumstances occurred at the same time. I had retired from public school teaching and was living on a fixed income. I had a tenant who was extremely uncooperative and then got an inspector who was beyond unreasonable. Not only did he fail the apartment, his list of changes was daunting—it seemed like he wanted the whole place renovated! Repeated failures meant that I would receive no rent. My uncooperative tenant had been encouraging the inspector to find all the faults that he could then use to fail the apartment. She had figured out that if it failed often enough, she could live there rent free.

Fortunately, I had been receiving extensions of the Section 8 payment but these reprieves could not go on forever. I failed inspection after inspection — nine in a row! The inspector always managed to find some reason to fail the apartment. The possibility of not receiving my Section 8 payment was real, and that could cause a cascading financial catastrophe.

I had been chanting morning and evening but was discouraged each time I failed an inspection. I wondered if I was chanting vigorously enough. Maybe I wasn't sufficiently focused while I was chanting, or possibly I was not chanting long enough. The one thing I was certain of was that chanting was in some way going to help me through this dilemma.

Prior to the tenth inspection, I chanted vigorously and for prolonged periods of time. I visualized passing the inspection. I suppressed any fear. I went ahead with complete confidence that I was going to be successful. On the day of the inspection I waited outside in front of the building. I was calm. I was confident. I waited for the inspector to arrive as he had so many times before. But this time, a different car pulled up and a different inspector approached the house. I introduced myself. He informed me that he was conducting the inspection that day.

I told him about the nine previous inspections and the problems with my tenant. When we entered the apartment, she was shocked to see a different inspector and made her agitation apparent. He could see how angry she was, but moved through the apartment conducting a thorough inspection. She told him that one of the cabinet drawers was off its runners. He opened the drawer and discovered that it was over-packed with paper bags. He said, "Maybe you shouldn't have stuffed so many bags in there."

She was livid, and he seemed nervous, but made his notes and we left the apartment together. He said that he was concerned about my tenant's attitude but also, he told me that the previous inspector had a history of being out of control. He apologized for all I had been through with the other inspector and handed me the form indicating that the apartment had passed inspection.

From the experience with the building inspector and my tenant, I learned many things. First, that chanting is not an exact science. I failed nine inspections before reaching a depth in my practice that resulted in success but because I ultimately succeeded, the process validated my faith in my practice. It provided me with "actual proof" that chanting works. This reinforced my previous experiences of bringing my problems to the Gohonzon, and chanting deeply and vigorously for a way forward. I persevered and like the long-distance runner, realized my capacity. Throughout this process I was never afraid because I had complete faith that I would achieve my goal.

During my chanting, I often focus on one of my ancestors; usually, my mother or a more distant relative. I feel more at ease visualizing someone who is not a part of my daily life. I ask for support with what I am trying to achieve, either in the form of better insight or simply to be successful in my endeavor. Sometimes just the calmness that follows chanting is enough to enable me to see a clearer solution. Sometimes, against all odds, I have a breakthrough.

Problems to which chanting does not immediately provide a solution frequently have proven to be more complex than I thought. In those instances, results have occurred in a different manner and usually over a longer period of time. The results can be obvious or subtle; usually involving changes in others or in me.

My Butsadan

For example, on one occasion I needed a new car. My then present car, although very nice, was 12 years old. It became cost prohibitive to make the repairs necessary to pass annual inspection, so I chanted for a new car. Not a brand-new car but one that was only a couple of years old. I chanted arduously and I envisioned the car that I wanted. I was very clear with regards to what I wanted to achieve. But over a period of time, I did not see my desired results. Steadfastly, I continue to chant.

At some point in the process I realized that I should prepare for getting this car. I was surprised when I checked my credit report and found that things that I had paid off were still listed. I began resolving those matters and thereby improving my credit score. As I continued to chant I realized it might be beneficial to visit the dealership at which I envisioned purchasing the car. I began to talk with one of the salesmen. I informed him of my dream car and all of the requirements. Slowly things began to improve.

One day I stopped by the dealership simply to "kick the tires" of the car that I wanted. I spoke with the salesmen and inquired about the possibility of being ready to make a purchase. In essence, I had chanted vigorously and consistently and was successful in purchasing the exact car that I wanted within $20 of the monthly payment that I had chanted for. The unexpected benefit of this experience was that I cleaned up issues that were on my credit report. I gained reliable transportation I needed for work purposes. Indeed, I improved the depth and consistency of my practice and gained "actual proof" of its effectiveness. Although this was a material benefit, it set the stage for realizing more important and long-lasting life improvements.

I have no idea where these solutions, support or guidance come from but I wonder if it's from some force that's been with me all my life. I have experienced this force many times and have consequently been able to calm my fears—the fear of failure and of losing what I have achieved.

My liturgy book, bell and beads

I believe that chanting from deep within my body, with resonance and conviction, may create a harmonic that brings me into better alignment with the universe. This harmonic, which in other forms of Buddhism is sometimes referred to as "throat singing," is thought to bring the practitioner in tune with the universe. Chanting is arduous, requiring some time to bring my full being into alignment. Upon reaching a certain level of calmness I feel a fusion with my Gohonzon, because it represents the various aspects of my life.

One of the central foundations of Buddhism is Shakyamuni's teaching of the Eightfold Path, known as the Middle Path or simply stated The Middle Way. The Middle Way on the surface seems a simple teaching of not being excessive in anything. But, the question of excessive actually lies with the individual. Excessiveness is a state of mind based on the level of drive to obtain or keep a thing. Once a person reaches mindset of being consumed by the need for a thing, that drive has become excessive and is outside of the Middle Way.

As one might expect, the concept of excessiveness has evolved not only during the passage of time but additionally as Buddhism has spread through various cultures and economic strata. Thus, a person striving for a Mercedes Benz car may well be within the Middle Way if that striving does not cause financial hardship or is the result of excessive desire. Indeed, having several well-made suits may be thought of as being excessive in one society but a basic requirement in another.

By chanting Nam-myoho-renge-kyo, which literally means "devotion to the mystic law of cause and effect through sound," I have been able to reach a level of consciousness that allows me to be in harmony with my environment. At those times, the clarity that enables me to understand the delusions and faulty perceptions comes from within me. I can choose to improve or continue to make life choices based upon the delusions and faulty perceptions.

Within the construct of my Buddhist practice I believe that I am a part of everything and everything is a part of me. That is about the most simplistic explanation that can be made about what is actually a very profound and difficult way to conceive reality. This is the Myoho, or the mystic aspect of chanting. It is like trying to imagine the end of infinity only to realize there is no end or beginning and one must conceive of things in a different paradigm. Inherent in my being is the potential for the best of me to be manifest. Alternately, there is the potential for me to go through my life making decisions based upon delusions and faulty information that were intentional, or not made a part of my life by living in the environment in which I was born. In Buddhism we believe that we choose to be born into situations that allow us to challenge those issues that we had not resolved in previous lifetimes. Those unresolved issues are impediments to achieving enlightenment. I can fully embrace my state of original enlightenment in this lifetime.

Through my practice, I have been fortunate to realize that the origins of our problems trace back to delusions and the fundamental darkness that has prevented the recognition of our inherent enlightenment through many lifetimes. It must be that all of the experiences I have had prior to encountering Nichiren Buddhism have prepared me for this practice. I prefer this to praying to an unseen entity and hoping that those things that challenge me from being the best that I can be are somehow resolved by this outside force.

Paul's Transmigration

My cousin Paul was approximately my age — a small-framed, handsome man. He lived in the Ruggles Street project until moving to an apartment only two blocks away. Like all of us, he started going to parties as a teenager. Part of the party routine was drinking. It helped to calm the nerves and provided relaxation as you danced.

This was not social drinking but rather passing the liquor bottle around and drinking straight out of the bottle. It was the same kind of drinking my uncles engaged in after working in the factory, the same kind of drinking that leads to alcoholism.

When Paul returned from his enlistment in the Air Force it was evident he had a drinking problem. No one knows when it occurred — it was probably a gradual development. He maintained his own apartment and always had a job, although he never married. When he grew older, Paul was the one who would visit the old folks to make sure they had groceries. He would call to see how things were going but when he called, I could always tell that he was under the influence of alcohol.

After years of abusing his body Paul developed cirrhosis of the liver. Over a period of time, he was required to have several serious operations, but I had no idea he was close to death. At some point in his decline he began to go to church. One day I received a telephone call informing me that Paul had died. This was a big shock, because he was the first in our age group to pass away.

When I went to the funeral I barely recognized him. He had been a fair-skinned man but the person in the coffin was blue-black. I was informed he had died alone in his apartment and it had been several days before he was discovered. Apparently, he had struggled prior to dying. Paul's passing was sad and tragic.

There is a section in my morning Gongyo that is a prayer for the deceased. You sound the bell continually while visualizing those you are focusing on. In this way you support them by directing energy their way. In this way, you tap into the myoho aspect of the practice. For years, I envisioned about 17 friends and family members who had died, directing my prayers to them. The list included my mother, my Aunt Blanche, my grandparents and a number of friends. I very much like the idea of being able to support those who have gone before me and are no longer with us.

In one instance, my mother had come to me after her passing, bringing a message of comfort and relief. Shortly after her death, my mother-in-law came to me. Again, with the message that everything was going to work out. Each time this occurred, the person's form was very much present in the room. These were exceptional experiences in my life, and confirmed to me that there is much more going on in this existence than I understand.

Not long after his death, Paul came to me in a dream. Again, this was totally unexpected as I had not been thinking about him in any way. We were in what I recognized as a the second floor of a government building with a stone floor, marble columns, and wrought iron railings surrounding a view to the lower level.

I saw Paul on the other side of the room. He looked small and was wearing striped pajamas that reminded me of the photographs of prisoners in Auschwitz. His head was bent down and he was looking from side to side, hunched over, hugging himself. He looked fragile and confused.

I rushed over and held him in my arms. As I patted him on the back, I heard the thud of my hand. We never spoke and he never looked at me but our communication was expressed in feelings. I sensed he was frightened and confused. He had not transitioned to where he was going and was stuck in some place in between.

As I reflected on this experience, I felt the power of the transmission and that I was being reached out to and asked for help. Later that morning as I was doing Gongyo, I reached the prayer portion for the deceased. Rather than my usual visualizing of relatives grandparents and friends, I decided to focus on Paul. I visualized the experience and my emotions, and I chanted vigorously for Paul to transition smoothly to wherever he was going.

I focused on Paul not only during the prayer for the deceased but also during my chanting. I began chanting for a prolonged period of time and on a daily basis not only for the things that I was trying to achieve, but also for my cousin Paul.

This campaign of prayer and chanting went on for at least three months. Again, Paul unexpectedly came to me. Again, I was in the same ornate building on the second floor. However, this time we were on the same side of the room. As I turned to greet him, he was taller and larger, not the diminutive person I had seen before. He emitted an aura of confidence and was wearing a fashionable white suit. My sense is that Paul had transitioned to wherever he was going. I believe that the energy I put into the universe through chanting and prayer in some way aided in his transition. I feel that he is at peace.

As I continue my practice, I learn more and more of its power. I perform Gongyo twice a day, almost every day. I repeat the same sections diligently. As I evolve as a Buddhist, I have learned how to employ this practice in far more profound ways than I had ever thought possible and, as a result, I have evolved as a human being.

Refining Points

What we think, we become.
— Buddha

Until I was a teenager I had not traveled more than a mile away from my home. I did not have the benefit of parents who had traveled widely and could share those experiences. The culture that I had been brought up in had a very limited perspective. My morality and religious beliefs were based upon experiences gained in a very narrow setting.

Once I began to question this reality, I began to ponder my death. I wondered if there was any way I could escape it. I wondered if by some miracle that the earth and all its inhabitants could simultaneously come to an end so I would not be alone. The inevitability of death and my own mortality scared me. That was my first experience in thinking about anything in depth and questioning the validity of what I knew. This was the first time that I sought answers to perplexing questions. Ever since, the habit of in-depth thinking and questioning has prevailed in my life.

My first information about sex, for example, came from titillating hallway conversations in the apartment buildings where we lived. The other boys were not much older and had no more experience than I, but would simply lie. Consequently, my ideas were based on falsehoods and misconceptions. How many of us have gone through our lives with concepts based upon faulty information? And, as a result, have interacted with others based upon stereotypes, lies and delusions?

My first real questions were based upon a hard look at my church. My friend Phillip was planning to enter the priesthood. He was one of the hallway boys, talking about sex and young girls. As a result of some of our more intimate conversations, I knew some of the less flattering things he had done. Even though people can evolve, I had my reservations. I commended him on the choice to follow a spiritual path, but his decision provided the impetus for my questioning and finally leaving the church.

I confessed my first sexual encounters to a priest and was soundly chastised, receiving significant penance for my "sins." I wondered why what I did was so wrong. If sex is after all a part of human nature, why had I been so severely punished? Whether my thoughts were wrong at the time caused me to question the whole structure of the church. Too many of my questions were answered with the necessity to have faith. Too many mysteries went without receiving plausible answers. I wanted "actual proof." This questioning is known in Buddhism as having a "seeking mind." People with this mindset do not take things at face value.

As a young boy, I demonstrated the ability to do classwork at a segregated school. I then entered a high-ranking predominantly white high school. When I began high school, I had never been around any white people, and had seldom been in the company of anyone who had finished college. It is embarrassing, humbling and painful to remember my ignorance and prejudice.

During high school I changed dramatically. It was the tumultuous 1960s, and current events made me more aware of what was going on in the world. I was always a highly disciplined student, but the challenges brought by studying hard sciences enabled me to learn to think more abstractly and more profoundly. As I changed in response, my attitudes and behavior caused me to move further away from my community. Standing apart from the other neighborhood residents made me a target.

In fact, even living in my building at Lenox Street became precarious. A few others there were also trying to get a good education but many of the young men floated in and out of reform school as a rite of passage. Some developed lifelong alcohol and drug habits. Many attended school out of habit and did not prepare themselves for adulthood. Occasionally, I encounter some of the young men from my neighborhood performing work as day laborers and handymen. Once in a while I encounter them as plumbers or carpenters but that is seldom.

However, a few of the Lenox Street group that I grew up with went on to do interesting things with their life. Ronald Critchlow became a high official in the Boston public school system. Lawrence Peters developed as an outstanding guitar player. David Crowder became a successful realtor. This is just a sampling of the few people who I encounter that made their way beyond the norm of Lenox Street.

When I started at the University of Massachusetts in Boston, I got my first real apartment. I was also interacting with a more diverse population and was stimulated by the intellectual nature of the college experience. As far as I had come, I was questioning how far I had yet to go to become the person I wanted to be.

My academic development continued through graduate school and a doctoral program, paralleled by

professional growth and workplace experience. However, I was still plagued by a fundamental darkness. I wandered through various religious experiences and developed a life philosophy based on solitary thinking and interactions with a small group of friends. Although that philosophy evolved somewhat, I always adhered to it because it enabled me to make informed decisions and kept me out of trouble.

When I first encountered Buddhist literature, I was astonished at how much my philosophy aligned with Buddhist thought. Concepts I had been thinking about for many years were actually common to people who had lived long ago in faraway places. At last, I had a body of information to guide me. I felt confident that ideas I had not carried to their natural conclusions were carried out further in the literature, and were similar to what I might have eventually resolved. Buddhism presented me with a way of life and thinking that I could embrace. I did not have to wonder if my conclusions were based on ignorance, delusion or poorly-thought-out ideas. Since my practice has been paramount to my further development, I wonder if the things I need to learn in this life are refining points, overcoming obstacles I had not mastered previously, and using skills previously developed.

Even more intriguing were concepts that were counterintuitive. Although everything does not follow a linear progression, I was uncertain how that manifested in real life. I had no one to talk to about such abstract notions. As my study of Buddhist literature progressed I read about Shukyamuni Buddha in the Lotus Sutra. But the Lotus Sutra is a complex body of literature. For more than a millennium, Buddhist scholars such as Dengyo Daishi and T'ien-t'ai devoted their lives to providing clearer and deeper understanding of its words and concepts.

Standing upon the shoulders of these great thinkers is the 13th century sage Nichiren Daishonin. He provided further clarification to the ideas of Shukyamuni Buddha, and was a supreme scholar of Buddhism as well as a prolific writer. His guidance as the Buddha of the Latter Day is Nichiren Buddhism that I now practice.

Ripples in the Water

Winter always turns into Spring.
— Nichiren Daishonin

As a youngster during the warm months of the year and particularly during school vacation my favorite activity was swimming. I lived close to the ocean and could simply walk up to Northampton Street and catch the bus to City Point, an ocean cove located in South Boston. At that time, South Boston was notorious being off-limits to African-Americans but City Point seemed to be an exception.

Swimming in the Atlantic Ocean was fun. The smell of salt air, the roast beef sandwiches and fried clams at Kelly's Landing were always a great treat. But it had its limitations. More often than not, the water was cold and murky and of course there was no diving. The sea shells strewn at the water's edge were painful for bare feet. Therefore, much of the time I preferred swimming at the Cabot Street Bathhouse. I could walk there from home. The route was a little precarious because I had to skirt the Ruggles Street project. I walked through Madison Park to Ruggles Street and picked up the beginning of Cabot Street. Ruggles Street projects on my right was fully populated and relatively clean. The houses on Cabot Street were old often vacant, dilapidated clapboard wood frame, two-story houses. At the corner of Cabot and Ruggles Street was the ever-present variety store. My route was marked with spots that were now overgrown with weeds and strewn with debris where houses had once been.

Cabot Street Bathhouse, 1940s

The bathhouse was built in the style of traditional municipal buildings of stone, oak and wrought iron building materials. The entrance doors were huge and of heavy wood. The bathhouse was a two-story building with a round domed roof, its doors flanked by stone columns. Upon entering the building, you found yourself in a large open area. The entryway floor was made of Terrazzo stone and a curved stairway hugged the wall leading to the second floor. Although I seldom ventured upstairs, from the first floor I could hear the sounds of young men playing basketball. Many similar municipal buildings still survive, fully functioning in the Greater Boston area.

Upon entering the building, you would go to a large wooden desk, behind which was seated an attendant. The first thing you did was show the attendant that you had a towel. You paid a nickel to swim, signed the attendance sheet and made your way to the lower level.

Cabot Street Bathhouse Swimming Pool

Of course, the swimming pool was on the ground level downstairs. The downstairs area was flanked with rows of green metal lockers. There were wooden benches to sit on in order to undress and take a shower before going into the pool. Most of the boys swam naked. This might have been awkward during the hot summer months when the open entrance doors provided a clear view to the outside world. But no one seemed to care. The shower and locker area always smelled of high humidity. The pool released a smell of chlorine that permeated the entire building. As one always seems to hear in buildings with this construction, the echo of children laughing and hollering was ever present.

Sometimes instead of splashing around I would just hold my breath and float face down in the water. I felt very relaxed and in tune with the water. As I floated I could see the nearby ladders of the pool clearer. I noticed bubbles floating around me. Background sounds, if audible at all, were subdued. People and objects further away were blurry. As they came closer they became clearer. Floating in the pool was a sublime state of being.

Cabot Street Bathhouse foyer

Chanting takes me to this same state. When I chant, I feel as though I am floating. I have my eyes open and I can see the problems I'm dealing with. My body is calm as if in the water. When I look around, I can see in the distance whatever it is I am confronted with. The less clear I am about the issue, the more blurred it appears. As I become more in harmony with the universe, the concern comes into focus and I am able to gain a better understanding.

Chanting is like sending ripples out into the water. Those ripples, like cause and effect, return in the fashion in which they have been sent. If my chanting is confused, chaotic and negative that is what returns. The more clarity I achieve on my requests, the more effective my chanting becomes. One who is untrained or unaware can unwittingly envision the most negative things about themselves and put them out into the universe only to have them return in like fashion.

One of my goals is to become a calmer, emotionally stronger person. The youthful volatility or urban edginess that initially enabled me to survive was a hindrance to my development as someone harmonious and in tune with his environment. As I have grown, I have gained control, although some ways of being remain ingrained. Some doors may have been closed, some people may have judged me before getting to know me. It is like being a tuning fork out of harmony with the environment and therefore unable to add as much value to life as may have been otherwise possible.

During the process of chanting, I reach a certain level of calmness and serenity. If I achieve fusion with the Gohonzon, I no longer see the scroll. My vision goes inward, my breathing slows. I don't hear or even notice the repetitions. I continue chanting, at ease and in peace for prolonged periods of time, drilling deeper into myself. I reach a point of contentment, almost euphoria. I enjoy this state of being and chant longer. As I chant longer I confront and defeat more issues and move closer to my goal of serenity. I have found that the words that emanate from my body as I chant are like a harmonic vibration, bringing me more in tune with the environment.

Depending upon the situation of the day and my state of mind, I may approach my practice calmly or in a state of agitation. I may approach my Gohonzon with just the concerns of the upcoming day or with a nagging, troubling, problem of great perplexity. But after chanting for a period of time, I reach a level that is equivalent to floating in a swimming pool and everything seems manageable.

As I have become more proficient in my practice, my chanting has become more focused, more positive and more powerful. What you put out into the universe is what returns to you. In Buddhism this is called making a "cause." When you determine what you want to achieve, you have made a cause. Chanting steadfastly to achieve that cause will enable every thought, every action and every part of your body to move in that direction. When you chant and infuse with the Gohonzon you more effectively invoke the powers of the universe, mindful that the universe does not operate on the same timetable as we sentient beings. Additionally, what you are trying to achieve may be far more complex than you realize. What you receive as a result of your chanting may initially elude your comprehension. It is critically important to comprehend the benefits of your practice and to show appreciation. We show appreciation by recognizing results of our practice and by chanting for others and their well-being.

In Buddhism we believe that the solutions to your problems are within you, although a direct answer itself may not be there. Rather, you may have the resources to obtain the answer or solution. The larger view is that we are, individually and collectively, a part of everything and everything is a part of us. We exist in harmony with the greater universe and therefore as the problems come to us, so do the solutions. Within the practice of chanting and making a cause that ripples out into the universe, we may experience an instantaneous resolution or solution to whatever it is that plagues us.

I have come to realize that in the greater universe, time does not operate in the same way as in our lives. In my understanding of the complex nature of time in the greater universe events influence occurrences on a multitude of levels, including past, future, and the present. These influences gain further complexity by impacting the emotional, cognitive, physical, and psychic components of our life. A feeling or smell or thought that we had as a child may come to full understanding much later in life. But does that smell, thought or feeling transcend previous lives and blend into future lives? I believe it does. Therefore, it is possible and most likely some of the things we chant for in this lifetime may not manifest themselves until another lifetime. This means that it is most likely that things we sought to improve by putting energy into the universe through chanting in previous lifetimes will manifest themselves now, or possibly in the future. The implications are very pleasing and give pause to much thought.

As I float in the calmness inherent in chanting, I am able to bring my issues into focus. In a deeper, more directed chant I don't hear background noise that could bring me out of this state. Instead, an issue that seems far away, blurry and difficult to comprehend, moves closer and becomes clearer. Once I better understand the problem, I am better able to envision a solution. Often my initial understanding of the problem will change, commonly referred to as a "paradigm shift" and I am able to explore both problems and benefits from various perspectives. I have found that my understanding of both problems and benefits are enhanced by the ability to embrace them from the various points of view that are achieved while chanting.

As I have become more proficient at chanting and developed a better understanding of the state that emerges as I chant, I have been able to deflect many of the karmic issues that only appear to distract me. These issues are a part of my life, but within my practice they have been reduced to an increasingly minor part of my life. They no longer serve as distractions that keep me from evolving into the more harmonious and in tune with the universe person that I strive to become. As I float in the calm atmosphere that emerges when I chant, the concerns along with the joys become clearer to me. How I appreciate the joys and how I handle the concerns emerge from within me.

As I have deflected, reduced, and overcome minor karmic issues I have been left with only the most plaguing and difficult of my issues. In Buddhism these issues are known as the "fundamental darkness." They are the core issues you may have been dealing with, lifetime after lifetime. The minor distractions that emerge in your sublime state of chanting give way to this major issue that has to be dealt with in order to reach your highest state of being. It's as if during chanting, a great glob of darkness simply appears from time to time, but it is always there in the background.

The reality is the more you chant and reach the tranquil level available to you, the more proficient you become at reaching and staying within that state of being. You feel good in this realm and the tendency is to be able to and want to chant longer and more profoundly. The minor karmic issues dissolve, leaving only bedrock and fundamental issues of your existence. That is not to say that our daily concerns cease to exist, but rather that those concerns no longer impede your progress in the human revolution. However, a steadfast and disciplined practice is required to defeat the fundamental darkness that has pursued you through many lifetimes.

Most of us hardly recognize the various levels of being in which we exist. The most obvious and universal example is the many worlds we have access to when we dream. Another example, experienced by a small number of people, are the levels of existence accessed through mediums such as athletics, dance, music and song.

The dancer, dancing alone, with a partner or in a group feels the power of existing within the plane of the dance. When shared, the dancer's experience and abilities are enhanced by those of another and the dynamics of the shared experience grow exponentially. Similarly, we see the musician's rapture, whether in opera, a church group or a popular music, experiencing existence on another plane accessed by singing or playing their instruments and exploring the nuances of their craft. The athlete, pushing his body to the utmost limit, reaches a level unexplainable to those who have not experienced it. These are some of the ways in which we can access some of the many levels of existence.

Chanting Daimoku is one way to access all the levels of our existence. Just as the dedication of the singer, artist, dancer and athlete take effort to achieve their goals and thereby experience life on a different plane. Chanting also takes practice and dedication. However, unlike bodily perfection or entertainment, the goal of chanting is much higher. By chanting we can obtain happiness. By chanting we can alleviate the pain and suffering inherent in this existence. Chanting alone is a powerful experience. Some of us chant alone because it eliminates time constraints, pacing, and other idiosyncratic concerns. Chanting in a group, on the other hand, adds incredible harmonics, power and focus and the power in numbers when chanting can never be underestimated.

So many of us go through life repeating the same mistakes and falling into the same traps. How much better would be the quality of our lives if we didn't stumble through blindly? Chanting gives us access to a level of being that enables us to obtain enlightenment. This enlightenment, however, does not mean that we will be able to understand Einstein's theory of relativity, nor fully grasp quantum physics. It does mean that we will not make the same mistakes over and over again. Once enlightened, those errant decisions and stumbles we have made over and over again become obvious. Enlightenment gives us the opportunity to avoid pitfalls and thereby improve the quality of our lives. It opens our eyes to the patterns of our existence. Once we are cognizant of these patterns we can see the benefits and deficits that emerge.

When friends and family members ask, "What has happened? You're so much calmer, less edgy." I smile. They have noticed a change, a calmness, a serenity. This is the direct result of my Buddhist practice. I am moving toward being the person that I envision myself to be. It is at this time that I share with them the benefits of my Buddhist practice.

Peace and Comfort

The three core components of the practice of Nichiren Buddhism are: chanting the mantra Nam-myoho-renge-kyo, which expresses key concepts of the law of life that all Buddhist teachings in some way seek to clarify; studying the teachings of Nichiren and making an effort to share the teachings of Buddhism.

My daily practice consists of sitting on a small bench while reciting portions of the Lotus Sutra (referred to as the liturgy or Gongyo, while chanting Nam-myoho-renge-kyo (referred to as Daimoku) in front of a mandala (the Gohonzon). This routine can be arduous and requires discipline, but the rewards are tremendous. Like most Americans, I have both daily tasks and long-term responsibilities involving family, health, work and investments, all of which can be challenging. At earlier periods in my life I would mull over such problems while driving to work or trying to fall asleep at night, and consequently would begin my workday stressed or plagued by racing thoughts. Through my practice, I have established a rhythm, not only in my home but also in my life that has enabled me to cope with these challenges.

I wake up at approximately the same time every morning. As an important part of beginning my day, and the essence of my practice, I do morning Gongyo. I sit before my Gohonzon and chant for a period of time, perform Gongyo and chant some more. I change the water in the cup that is part of the symbols that are housed in my Gohonzon. To me, the water symbolizes, in part, the eternal, formless reality of life. I usually have fresh fruit present, symbolizing the need for nutrients that sustain life. I burn incense; usually, a sandalwood gum that is long-lasting and very fragrant. Next to my Gohonzon I have a medium-sized round bell that I strike during certain portions of Gongyo. The resonation of the bell is intended to penetrate the unknown aspects of this existence.

My juzu beads also have symbolic meaning. Over the course of time, the configuration of two tuffs on one end and three on the other has come to represent man. The garland of beads represents eternity as a never-ending loop. Individual beads may vary in size and material, and have numerous traditional meanings.

This collection of traditional objects and symbols used in my practice is soothing. The scented air, though not essential, creates a reminder of previous practices. The sound of the bell followed by Daimoku creates a sense of harmony and establishes the rhythm of the practice. These rituals have helped me to gain confidence, particularly on days potentially fraught with challenge. Often after a period of time chanting Daimoku, which inevitably calms my mind, solutions to these daily challenges have found their way into my thoughts. I have not forced these thoughts but rather have allowed my mind to present options, even if the option was only to remain calm.

Chanting Daimoku is not meant to be a stress-laden vehicle for achieving breakthroughs or shifting paradigms. On the contrary, it is a way of becoming in tune with yourself, your thoughts and your potential. It is also a recognition that not all of your endeavors are going to work out as planned. Some may be prototypes for future ventures; some, for reasons as yet unknown, may not be in your best interest.

At approximately the same time every evening I perform Gongyo as a means of closing my day. Evening Gongyo gives me a variety of opportunities, such as the occasion to express thanks for the day's achievements. I am also able to contemplate things that did not go so well. Most of all, I am able to unwind from the day's events.

Once a week I meet with area group members for study and chanting. During these meetings we discuss the philosophical foundations of Nichiren Buddhism by exploring the many writings of Nichiren Daishonin. Once we choose a study topic it becomes the basis of inquiry and group conversation.

Finally, on Sunday mornings there is the opportunity to perform Gongyo at the area cultural center. Whereas we most often meet in our districts or local communities this is an opportunity to meet with a larger group of practitioners. These meetings are also used as one might expect for conferring awards, welcoming new members as special occasion activities.

Between the individual practice and group meetings, a certain rhythm is established. Although regular attendance at the local meetings is encouraged, members have the option to participate more and take on greater responsibility. Over time, I have gradually tailored my hectic and demanding life around my practice and meetings. As a consequence, I do not work late on the nights that we have local meetings. I also find time to read and explore the indepth aspects of this spirituality. And as a result I have found more peace and comfort in my life.

Did the Buddha Speak to Me?

The historical Buddha, Shakyamuni was grown, married and had a child when he began his quest for knowledge some 2,500 years ago in India. Ultimately, it is a universal message that transcends the past, present and future. Shakyamuni was in the right place at the right time for his teaching to be preserved. Most likely others with such clear insights have come and gone unnoticed. Some few, such as Mohammed and Jesus Christ, were in the right time and the right place for their insights about particular aspects of our existence to have been preserved.

But did Shakyamuni speak to my reality as an African-American man, who in fact is mixed with many people who did not exist as a people in his time. The complexity of identity and sociological issues that confront me did not exist 2,500 years ago. Have black people followed in the steps of the currently dominant European culture, to the exclusion of their own philosophical, theosophical voice? Have we denigrated those who may have presented clarity with regards to our existence in favor of the religions and theosophy of the European?

We can liken the theosophy made available throughout time to the songs sung in some great opera of clarity throughout an eternal time. The theme of the opera has been sung to the audience by gifted philosophers on a grand stage covering time and locations. There were opening songs presented by lesser philosophers, but those songs were critical to set the stage. The theme, the insights, the clarity in the original opera has been reinterpreted. The reinterpretations are embellishments and reformatted aspects of the grand opera, to address the times, locations and needs of the current audiences.

But do the songs delivering the teachings and insights of Shakyamuni resonate with me? After all, for more than 400 years, my native culture has more closely aligned with that of Europe. If the opera "The Buddha" was presented with an exclusively Asian cast, would I attend a presentation? Even more so, would I more likely attend the opera "Mohammed?" This production was cast with people who look more like me.

Finally, I wondered if I would more than likely attend the opera "Jesus Christ Superstar." The production is phenomenal. It is advertised everywhere. I know that the current production does not feature characters that look like me, but the original production did. My lineage as far back as I can trace has attended productions of this opera.

The metaphor of an opera is used as a way to address the challenges confronting any group of people who step outside of their comfort zone to participate in a religion with which they do not readily identify on a racial level. On a grander stage, we should be paying attention to the message and not the color, place of origin or social standing of its bearer. Unfortunately, as compelling and insightful as that message may be, we seem to overwhelmingly look for someone with whom, for a variety of superficial reasons, we can identify. Therefore, if we perceive the church, cultural center, synagogue or mosque as belonging to those not of us we tend not to embrace the message or go to hear the message. Unless we are Indian or Chinese, few of us might venture into the Chinese or Indian houses of worship down the street. Maybe this is a phenomenon based on natural sociological grouping, but in a context that rises above racial characteristics, we are incredibly limiting our ability to embrace enlightenment that may ultimately resonate with our experience.

The enlightenment of the historical Buddha rises above the times and locations in which they have their origins. The uniqueness of his gift is that it addresses all of mankind throughout the ages with profound messages and insights about our existence. Undoubtedly these ideas have been pondered and unraveled by others and lost for a variety of reasons. Other profound insights that have survived have predominantly focused on how to live your life. The teachings of Shakyamuni were presented over 40 years and address virtually every aspect of our lives. During his life Shakyamuni reflected upon his earlier teachings and refined them.

His most comprehensive Sutra, the Lotus Sutra sits on the shoulders of many years of his enlightened teachings. It presents a profound insight to our complex existence and is available to all mankind. With all humility, yes, The Buddha did speak to me.

Buddhism: A Brief Timeline

- **Shakyamuni Buddha** (5th or 6th Century B.C.) The founder of Buddhism.

- **Kumarajiva** (China, 343/344 – 413 A.D.) One of the greatest Buddhist sutra translators in China. Born in Kucha, Kumarajiva studied with Hinayana masters before he was converted to Mahayana Buddhism. Well known as a great Buddhist master even as a young man.

- **T'ien-tiai** (surnames Chih-i, Chih-k'ai) (China, 531-597 A.D.) Systematized the teachings implicit in the Lotus Sutra. Created a difficult, time-consuming, cumbersome, yet effective system of meditation for their realization.

- **Dengyo Daishi** (surname Saicho) (Japan, 767 – 822 A.D.) Brought T'ien-t'ai Buddhism to Japan (Tendai sect). Unfortunately, the Tendai sect after Dengyo's death, through a series of events, became mixed with Pure Land Buddhism. Dengyo's writings in the Ebyo Shu were forgotten by all but a few minor teachers, and were not taken seriously again until the monk Nichiren came along.

- **Hui-Yuan** (China, 337 – 417 A.D.) founder of Pure Land Buddhism. Pure Land capsulated Buddhism, making it accessible to ordinary working people. But it taught that happiness in this world was impossible and could be found only in death, thus sapping peoples' determination, vitality and potential. This school emphasizes meditation to see the Pure Land (the land we go to when we die, a western paradise, purity revealed in enlightenment) and Amitabha Buddha. Founded by Hui-yuan ca. 402 C.E, the oldest and least philosophical school of Mahayana Buddhism in China.

- **Honen** (Japan, 1173-1212 A.D.): is one of the most outstanding figures in the long history of Japanese Buddhism. Along with Dogen, Nichiren and Shinran, his disciple, he represents the core of the revolutionary Kamakura Buddhist movement which created the first popular and uniquely Japanese forms of Buddhism. Though not as noted in the West than these counterparts, Honen is perhaps the most pivotal of the four since he was the first to break with the established centers of Tendai (T'ien T'ai) and Shingon (tantric) patronized by the royal court and military authorities. It was at age 43, with a deepening exposure to the Pure Land teachings of the great Chinese Master Shan-tao (Zendo), that Honen made this radical break to pursue his own spiritual vision.

- **Nichiren Daishonin** (Japan, 1222 – 1282 A.D.): Nichiren was a monk in the Tendai School. He became frustrated by the many paths of salvation that were taught, and left the Tendai monastery in search of the true Buddhist path. Eventually he condensed the Tendai practice, making it accessible to ordinary working people. Nichiren's studies led him to conclude that the Lotus Sutra contained the only true way to salvation and that chanting the phrase Nam-myoho-renge-kyo ("salutation to the Lotus Sutra") is the way to attain enlightenment. He founded the Nichiren School of Buddhism; wrote the Gosho, letters to his followers, now the primary study material for believers. Nichiren defined the universal law permeating life and the universe as Nam-myoho-renge-kyo and embodied it in the form of a mandala. In the Butsudan, a scroll on which are inscribed Chinese and Sanskrit characters, Nichiren symbolically depicted the life state of Buddhahood, which all people possess.

Glossary

Butsudan — A cabinet that enshrines and protects the Gohonzon, literally means House of the Buddha.

Cause — A determination to achieve something that is accomplished by performing Gongyo and chanting Daimoku.

Daimoku — Chanting Nam-myoho-renge-kyo.

Daisaku Ikeda — The third president of the Soka Gakki

Fundamental Darkness — Ignorance, sometimes called primal ignorance, within us all. A persistent and deceptive illusion, it is at times hard to ignore and it is also difficult to identify.

Gohonzon — A scroll housed in the Butsudan. Some of the characters on the Gohonzon are historical persons, mythical figures or Buddhist gods. Nichiren used them to represent the actual functions of the universe and of our own lives. All these functions are clustered around Nam-myoho-renge-kyo; therefore, the Gohonzon is the embodiment of the life of Buddhahood within us.

Gongyo — The Japanese word literally means "assiduous practice." In the practice of Nichiren Buddhism it means reciting Nam-myoho-renge-kyo, and portions of the second chapter Expedient Means and the sixteenth Life Span chapters of the Lotus Sutra in front of the Gohonzon. This is the fundamental practice of Nichiren Buddhism, which is performed morning and evening.

Juzu beads — A string of about 108 beads that Buddhists use to keep count of prayers.

Lotus Sutra — One of many sutras taught by Shakyamuni wherein he states the attainment of enlightenment is a possibility for all people, without distinction based on gender, race, social standing or education.

Nam-myoho-renge-kyo — Devotion to the mystic law of cause and effect through sound. (very brief literal explanation)

Nichiren Daishonin — Nichiren was born in 1222 in Japan. His study of the Buddhist sutras convinced him that the Lotus Sutra contained the essence of the Buddha's enlightenment. Based on his study of the sutra Nichiren established the invocation (chant) of Nam-myoho-renge-kyo as a universal practice to enable people to manifest the Buddhahood inherent in their lives.

Shoten Zenjin — Those powers in the universe that serve to protect us.

Soka Gakki — A group of lay practitioners practicing Nichiren Buddhism.

About the Author

Meikle Paschal, Ed.D. was born and raised in the South End of Boston, Massachusetts. He attended Boston Public Schools and earned his diploma from Boston Technical High School.

Dr. Paschal earned a Bachelor of Arts undergraduate degree, dual major in Psychology and English from University of Massachusetts at Boston. Later he completed a M.Ed. program from Cambridge College. He obtained a Master's Degree in English from Bridgewater State College. Finally, he completed a doctoral program at University of Massachusetts at Lowell and received the degree of Doctorate in Education with a major in Education Leadership. Along the way he obtained a teaching certification in English, supplementing the initial certification with principal licenses for the high school, middle school and elementary school levels.

Before becoming an administrator in the Boston Public School System he was the Director of Roxbury Enrichment Services a Non-resident alternative education facility. The bulk of his career has been spent in the field of education. Dr. Paschal worked in the Boston Public School System primarily as an administrator performing various duties i.e., Specialist, Assistant Principal and Director of Curriculum and Instruction. As his career advanced he worked at many area colleges and universities: Fitchburg State, Framingham State, and Curry College, in the area of Educational Leadership teaching various courses on the Graduate and C.A.G.S. levels.

After retiring from the Boston Public School system, Dr. Paschal continued teaching. Currently he teaches a variety of courses in English, Literature, Philosophy and Skill Development. Dr. Paschal's current teaching addresses his passion for working with underprepared and learning challenged students at Bunker Hill, MassBay and Middlesex Community Colleges. He developed the Academic Support for Athletes Program (A.S.A.P.) at Massbay Community College. In addition to his teaching responsibilities he holds the position of Academic Advisor to MassBay's student athletes.

Dr. Paschal is the founder and director of Metropolitan Educators Association (M.E.A.) in affiliation with Fitchburg State College. M.E.A. provides graduate courses, professional development training and other services to area educators.

Dr. Paschal's passion is working with non-traditional underprepared students. He is the father of five children: Aleta, Kendall, Kolette, Zakia, and Meikle, Jr. He currently resides in Lexington, Massachusetts with his wife Marilyn.